DAILY ⊚ NEWS
presents

Yogi Berra:
An
American Original

Sports Publishing Inc.
Champaign, IL

Director of Production: Susan M. McKinney
Interior Design: Michelle R. Dressen
Project Manager: Jennifer L. Polson
Coordinating Editors: Joseph J. Bannon, Jr., and Joanna L. Wright
Cover Design: Joe Buck

Front cover: photo from Photo Files
Back cover: photo by Mike Albans, *Daily News*

ISBN: 1-58261-339-7

Printed in the United States.

SPORTS PUBLISHING INC.
804 North Neil Street
Champaign, IL 61820
www.SportsPublishing.com

Acknowledgments

There are literally hundreds of people at the *Daily News* whose hard work and dedication throughout the past five decades have made this book possible. The efforts of the many reporters, columnists, editors, executives, photographers, librarians, and illustrators were all essential in bringing the incredible career of Yogi Berra to life every day in the pages of the newspaper.

When we first approached the *Daily News* about this project, we enjoyed the enthusiastic support of Les Goodstein (Executive Vice President/Associate Publisher) and Ed Fay (VP/Director of Editorial Administration), who ensured that we were given full access to the paper's unmatched resources. From then on, we received invaluable cooperation and assistance from Bill Madden, who covered Yogi and steered us through Yogi's amazing life; Bill Martin, Vincent Panzarino, Mike Lipack, Eric Meskauskas and Angela Troisi, who guided us through the most extensive archive of Berra photos in existence; Johnathan Moses and John Polizano, who contributed more than just their legal and business expertise; Faigi Rosenthal, Dawn Jackson, and Scott Browne, who helped us pore through the *Daily News* library files; and Lori Comassar and Lenore Schlossberg, who made sure we got the support we needed. A special thanks goes to Leora Harris, whose final editing and proof-reading were invaluable.

Space limitations preclude us from thanking each writer and photographer whose work appears in this book. However, wherever available, we have preserved the writers' bylines and the photographers' credits to ensure proper attribution for their work.

At Sports Publishing Inc., we are grateful for the support of Jennifer Polson, Susan McKinney, Joe Buck and Terry Hayden.

Although we have already acknowledged their professional contributions to this project, personal thanks go to Jenn, Billy, Vinny and Dawn for enjoying Yogi with us.

Joseph J. Bannon, Jr.
Joanna L. Wright
Coordinating Editors

Contents

Introduction

Yogi Berra is both an American icon as well as an American original. It has been said of him, in all accuracy, that he is the most recognizable figure in America. If Yogi were asked what he thought of all these accolades, he would probably say something like "if people want to say things about you, you can't stop them."

The fact is people have been saying nice things about Yogi Berra for over 50 years, ever since he came out of the Navy and broke into the major leagues with the New York Yankees as a squat, funny-looking outfielder/catcher in 1946. Throughout his half-century in baseball as a player, coach, manager, Hall of Fame Veterans Committee member and overall good-will ambassador, the *New York Daily News* has chronicled him. The highlights of those *Daily News* accounts of Yogi's career are gathered here in this book.

Even Yogi would have to admit, it's been a great ride, with mostly ups to it. As arguably the most important player on 10 Yankee world championship teams, Yogi won three Most Valuable Player Awards (1951, '54 and '55) and routinely caught over 145 games per year. His post-playing career as a manager was almost as successful as he twice took teams to the seventh game of the World Series—the Yankees in 1964 and the Mets in 1973.

Meanwhile, all along the way there have been those marvelous Yogiisms that have marked him as one of our great philosophers. He has told us it is never over 'til it's over and who could ever dispute that? He has warned us about certain restaurants being places where nobody goes anymore because they're too crowded. He advised us to take the fork in the road when we come to it, and he's told us on numerous occasions how 90 percent of baseball is half mental. I will always remember a breakfast I once had with Yogi in Cleveland that wound up costing me $25, even though I only had an English muffin, juice and some coffee. Yogi explained to me in complete seriousness, "they've got to import those muffins."

I'm sure I'm not alone in saying it's been a fabulous half-century just being around Yogi, watching him as a player hit one "bad ball" after another for game-winning home runs and later just listening to him offer his observations on the game and American life. Fortunately, all of Yogi through the years has been preserved in the stories, photos and cartoons of the *Daily News*. Here it is, as Yogi would say, "deja vu all over again" and if so much of the past is enjoyable it's only because "the future ain't what it used to be."

Bill Madden
New York Daily News

YOGI BERRA

"Bill Dickey learned me all his experiences."

1
1946-50: Becoming a Champion

	G	AB	R	H	2B	3B	HR	RBI	BB	SB	BA	SA
1946:	7	22	3	8	1	0	2	4	1	0	.364	.682
1947:	83	293	41	82	15	3	11	54	13	0	.280	.464
1948:	125	469	70	143	24	10	14	98	25	3	.305	.488
1949:	116	415	59	115	20	2	20	91	22	2	.277	.480
1950:	151	597	116	192	30	6	28	124	5	4	.322	.533

L awrence Peter Berra began his professional baseball career in Norfolk, Virginia, with the promise of $90 a month and a $500 signing bonus if he stayed with the Yankees' farm club for a full season. He left baseball more than four decades later with a Hall of Fame plaque and a resume that places him among the game's elite.

In between, Berra homered in his first major league game, anchored one of the greatest dynasties in sports, signed some of the most generous contracts of his time, and become known to all Americans simply as Yogi.

After rising through the minors primarily as an outfielder, Yogi initially split his major league time between the outfield and behind the plate. But under the tutelage of the great Bill Dickey, Yogi quickly became proficient with the "tools of ignorance," as the catcher's equipment was known. He became the Yankees' full-time catcher in 1949.

With Yogi behind the plate, the Yankees won every World Series they played for the next five years. ■

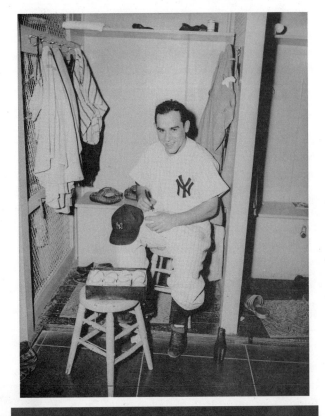

Yogi signs a baseball cap in the Yankees' dressing room during his rookie season.

November 18, 1964

Young Ideas

by Dick Young

(Shortly after Yogi's first stint as manager of the Yankees ended in 1964, Daily News *columnist Dick Young looked back on the events that had brought Yogi to the Yankees 20 years earlier.—Ed.)*

Yogi Berra likes money. I mean he likes it more than that, and the reason is something that happened almost 25 years ago, when the WPA in St. Louis was teaching baseball to a bunch of kids from The Hill.

The WPA, in case you grew up in this era of plenty, was something the government dreamed up during the Depression, before it was considered a disgrace to work for the relief money. The government created jobs for artisans, as well as for laborers, and at Sherman Park in St. Louis, this thing for kids kept physical training teachers and such busy, and kept the kids from snitching things at least for a few hours a day.

One of the kids at Sherman Park was named Yogi Berra, and another Joe Garagiola, and they played on different teams because Joey was a year younger than Yogi.

Terry Moore and Enos Slaughter and a few other Cardinal players would show up occasionally to help the kids, and scouts would drop by on the chance some raw talent might pop up. Dee Walsh was one of the scouts, and his eye was taken by the Garagiola kid.

Rickey Agreed to $500 for Garagiola

That summer, when school let out, Walsh talked Branch Rickey into signing Garagiola to a Cardinal farm contract for a $500 bonus, and everybody on The Hill was excited for Joey, including his buddy Yogi.

Meanwhile, another Cardinal scout, Jack Maguire, was trying to convince Rickey that the Berra kid was every bit as good as Garagiola, maybe better, but Rickey didn't believe it.

Fact is, Rickey said he had seen the Berra kid, and thought he was too clumsy and slow; that maybe he'd

Yogi with Joe Garagiola in the summer of 1947.

make triple-A, but not the majors. The highest Rickey said he would go for a kid like that was $250.

Maguire relayed the offer, and Larry Berra said no, nothing doing. Either he'd get the same $500 his pal Joey was getting to sign, or nothing. How would it look to Yogi's mother, anyhow, if she had to face Joey's mother every day, knowing her boy only got half as much to play ball.

Maguire sympathized with Yogi, to the extent that he tried to get a scout from the St. Louis Browns to give Yogi the five hundred. In those days, the Browns couldn't have given Joe DiMaggio $500, so Joey Garagiola went off to play professional ball at Springfield, Missouri, and Larry Berra went back to his job as tack puller at the shoe factory.

Weiss Heard About a Young Catcher

On weekends, the Berra kid would pick up a five- or ten-spot catching a game around town, and one day word got back to George Weiss in New York that there was a pretty good little catcher in St. Louis, and all he wanted was $500 to sign. It didn't matter how much a month pay, but it had to be $500 to sign. It was a thing with him.

Weiss sent Johnny Schulte to check on this Berra kid. Schulte was the bullpen coach for the Yankees and lived in St. Louis, so it was easy for him to visit the Berra home, and inexpensive. He didn't get to see Yogi play, but he talked with people who had, and when he offered $500, plus $90 a month to play with Norfolk in the Piedmont League, the Berra kid grabbed it. He was even, now, with his pal Joey, and that's all that mattered.

Berra reported to Norfolk, and started to wonder about the $500, because nobody had made a move to give it to him, and his father was starting to ask questions. Berra took the matter up with the general manager of the Norfolk club, and was told he wouldn't get the $500 unless he lasted out the season without getting cut.

Berra was stunned. He said that wasn't the way he understood it, but they showed him the small print, and that's what it said, so Yogi had to wait. He got the

Aaron Robinson, Ralph Houk, and Yogi Berra.
(News photo by Hank Olen.)

$500 at the end of the season, and he learned a lesson, too.

The scar left by that incident is told by him in *Yogi*, the excellent autobiography Ed Fitzgerald helped him punctuate a few years ago.

"When they gave me the business about not getting the money until I stuck with the ballclub for a year," Berra said, "I made up my mind I was going to see to it I got everything that was coming to me from then on. I think I have."

Yogi Always Recalled That $500 Item

Yogi was to sign a contract as high as $60,000 as he climbed to stardom with the Yankees. He drove his bargain hard, and held out at times, and always in the back of his mind was that they would never make him a sucker again, the way they did with that $500.

The Yankees have taken a rap on firing Berra as manager, and they're still taking it, but when you come down to it, Yogi was treated pretty well by them through the years, and even when they canned him as manager, they gave him a pretty sweet contract.

They signed him on as a scout at $25,000 a year, for two years, and said if he wanted to walk out at any time, to better himself, he could do it, and still get $25,000 in severance, and that kind of severance pay is Yankee class, whether you're sore at them or not.

Yogi isn't sore. They tried, at yesterday's press conference, to get him to say he was sore, or bitter, but Berra wouldn't say it.

"They were real good to me for 18 years," he said. "The Cards and Browns didn't want to sign me in my own hometown, but the Yanks signed me, sight unseen." ∎

WHAT'S IN A NAME?

While there are conflicting stories as to how Yogi earned his famous nickname, popular consensus is that he was tagged "Yogi" early on by his boyhood friends in St. Louis. The kids on The Hill had seen a movie in which one of the characters sat with his arms and legs folded in the Yoga position. Likening this picture to the way Berra sat on the bench, the "Yogi" moniker was born.

Reports that Berra was nicknamed after the Yogi Bear cartoon are off base. In fact, it was the other way around—the cartoon character was inspired by Berra.

Yanks Sweep Twin-Bill
Berra Homers in Debut
by Jim McCulley

September 23, 1946—Stoically situated in third place and going no place else this waning season, the Yanks tried out a couple of recruits from Newark against the Athletics in the first game of a Stadium doubleheader yesterday, and both rookies performed with acumen to hand Spud Chandler his 29th victory, 4-3. The Yanks also won the second game, 7-4. Darkness halted the game at the end of the sixth.

About 20,000 fans were present to watch shortstop Bobby Brown and catcher Larry (Yogi) Berra break into the major leagues in Yankee livery.

Berra, a 21-year-old ex-sailor who resembles Charlie Keller in stature and at bat, collected two hits in four trips. The second time up, in the fourth, he hit a home run with Keller on base which sewed up the victory for Chandler.

Brown, a 22-year-old former Tulane medical student, was flashy afield. He started a double play in the fifth which shut off a Philadelphia rally, ended the game with a great stop and throw, got one hit, and scored a run.

The Yanks banged out ten hits against the offerings of Jessie Flores and Bill McCahan in the opener. Berra's rap smashed into the lower bleachers in right and was hit off Flores. Chandler allowed the A's 10 hits, easing up after Berra's circuit blow had given him a 4-0 lead. The A's picked up a run in the fifth on three hits, duplicated the order in the sixth, and got another in the ninth.

October 7, 1947

Yanks Champs! Trim Flock, 5-2

by Joe Trimble

Yogi Wisdom

"Ninety percent of this game is half mental."

Brooklyn is a borough of three million pallbearers this morning. There, where the trees grow with equal vigor on the stately avenues of Flatbush and the sordid streets of Williamsburg, the citizens are deep in mourning. They've suffered their greatest loss—the world championship. With yesterday's 5-2 defeat in the seventh game of the Series, the dashing Dodgers died. They went down almost without a struggle under the crushing pitching of the Yankees' left-handed relief man, Joe Page, in the last of this mad set of games.

Page Mobbed by Team

The Dodgers last gasp came exactly at 3:49 in the bright sunshine which bathed the Stadium in glowing warmth. As McQuinn clutched the final throw, the Yanks poured from their bench and mobbed Page. They almost pulled his great left arm off and the right one, too. They grabbed and hugged him and finally swept him off the field before the fans could pour out of the seats and engulf him.

The championship was the 11th for the Yankees in 15 Series and their first since '43. It was a triumph for the new Yankee dynasty: president Larry MacPhail, who resigned after the game; manager Bucky Harris; and the players. For the disappointed Dodgers, this was

their fourth failure to win the title. They flopped in '16, '20, and '41. This was the first time they'd been able to carry it to a seventh game, however.

The crowd of 71,548 lifted the total attendance to a new Series record. Exactly 389,763 saw the seven sensational games and there must be at least that many ulcers in bloom.

The Dodgers began yesterday's game as if they intended to run off with the title before the Yankees even got to bat. Eddie Stanky poled a hard single in the first inning and then tried to steal second. He was nailed by Aaron Robinson's fine throw to Stirnweiss. Pee Wee Reese then walked and had larceny in his

For New York, Yankee rookie Frank Shea (14-5) will chuck and Yogi will be the man in the iron mask. (News photo by Walter Kelleher.)

heart, too. Robinson also cut him down with a swift peg to Rizzuto. The Brooks had previously stolen seven bases on the other Yankee catchers, but they found big, moody Robbie a rough customer. There wasn't a sign of theft after both were nabbed by the catcher's quick throws.

Yogi Misplays One

Robbie did more good throwing than Shea did in that inning and Frank's evident lack of stuff became more harmful to the Yanks in the second. He got Dixie Walker on a pop foul at the start of the frame, but was slugged for a triple to right by Hermanski. Yogi Berra, playing out there, wobbled like a drunk in a hurricane, as the ball caromed crazily off the low fence. It went one way and he went the other and he fell down. By the time he got up, the batter was safely on third. Yogi looked funnier than most of the comic book characters he enjoys.

As the Dodgers went to bat in the ninth, there was a swelling roar of anticipation. Many, many times previously this year they'd pulled games out of the fire. They'd even managed it with one hit after two were out in the ninth of this Series. With Dixie Walker leading off, the Faithful lighted little flickers of hope. But ol' Dix merely grounded to Stirnweiss. "Miksis'll fixus," they thought, and he tried with his solid whack. But Edwards rolled the ball to Rizzuto and that was the end.

So, as they have said in Brooklyn eternally, "Wait Till Next Year." ■

PAGE INTRODUCES 'LUCKY CHARM'

One smiling face stood out in the hilarious atmosphere of the Yankee dressing room after the Series clincher was applied. It belonged to 12-year-old Corky Chaill of the Bronx, who was introduced around by Joe Page as "my good luck charm."

It seems that Corky met Joe in the bullpen early in the season and has been sticking close ever since. As Corky puts it, "One day Joe said, 'I like you and want you to be my good luck boy.' And so I guess I have because he's been winning ever since."

One of Yogi's early roommates was Bobby Brown, who earned his M.D. and became president of the American League after retiring from baseball. One night Yogi finished his comic book, turned to Brown, who was reading a medical text, and asked, "How did yours come out?"

Berra's Thumb Ain't Good: He May Miss No. 3

October 7, 1949—Yogi Berra, the man who says funny things even if the news-papermen do make up most of them, isn't quite sure he'll be able to get back into the Yankee lineup with his big bat for today's third Series game. Flashing the swollen left thumb that kept him chained to the bench while his team was starving for a run yesterday, the Yankee slugger said: "It's worse than usual, so I'm not sure I can get ready this time."

As a rule Yogi's susceptible thumb, which puffs up after each painful effort behind the plate, reacts favorably to a one-day rest plus medication. But the punishment Berra took in working the first game evidently created greater damage than usual. "I had to swing the bat one-handed in practice today," he said with loud overtones of discouragement. "It ain't good."

"The only reason I need these gloves is 'cause of my hands."

THE GLOOM DESCENDS. Sidelined by a split in the webbing of his right hand, Yogi peers unhappily out at Yankee Stadium after the game was washed out. (News photo by Watson.)

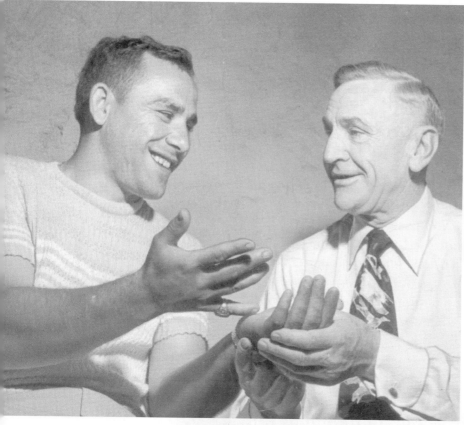

HOW'S THE PAWS? The double-threat hands of Yogi Berra (l.), Yank outfielder and catcher, pass Casey Stengel's inspection.

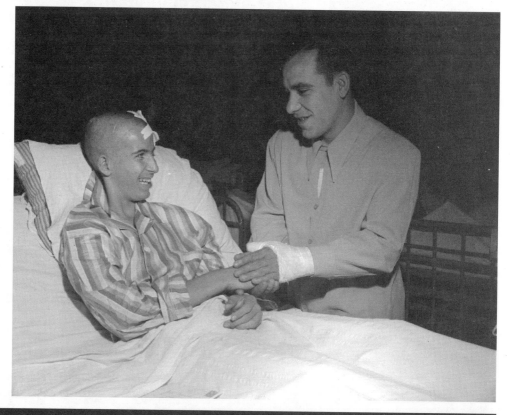

N.Y. Yankee catcher Yogi Berra shakes hands with 14-year-old Billy Maccard and wishes him a speedy recovery. Yogi injured his hand when he was hit by a baseball while batting. Billy himself stopped one with his head and was recuperating at Lincoln Hospital. (News photo by Tom Baffer.)

October 10, 1949

Yanks Win '49 Championship

Take 5th Series Game Under Arcs, 10-6

by Dick Young

By order of Commissioner Chandler, they turned the Ebbets Field lights on at 4:50 yesterday afternoon—but by that time none of the 33,711 fans who sat in on that unprecedented action could see the Brooks, anyway. They only saw the Yankees—who had by then wrapped up their 12th title by bloodying the NL challengers, 10-6.

The powerful arcs, used for the first time in a big league daytime tilt, were employed to cut the dusk that was gripping the field at the start of the final frame, but they served, just as much, to spotlight the mighty "Team of Destiny" in the same manner that Hollywood thespians are glamorized at big events.

Among those stars who made it look so easy by sweeping three straight to take the Series at four games to one, the night lights focused on Joe DiMaggio, who, snapping out of his pernicious slump, crashed a homer; on rookie Gene Woodling, who cracked three straight hits; on Vic Raschi, who came back to win on two days' rest and did a gritty job of it till he tired in the seventh; and, of course, on Joe Page, the inevitable Joe

Page, who ended the thing from the hill, just as he had done against the Dodgers two years before.

And, perhaps, some of the refracted light trickled onto a few Brooks—fellows like Gil Hodges who tried, but much too late, to keep his club alive with the three-run homer that routed Raschi, and Duke Snider, who ripped off his goatskin with three spectacular catches and two hits.

But Gil's circuit and Snider's grabs could not compensate for the extreme deficiency of the Dodger hurlers. This, the classic that was called the "Pitchers' Series" because of the overpowering hurling that

STRICTLY YANKEE TERRITORY. Front row (l. to r.): Mrs. Hank Silvera, Mrs. Johnny Lindell, and Mrs. Yogi Berra. Rear row (l. to r.): Mrs. Cliff Mapes and Mrs. Frank Scott. (News photo by Tom Baffer.)

marked the first two games, wound up as the "pitchers' series" because the Brooks used nothing but pitchers in trying to stop the flow of blood. Six moundsmen, as many as had ever been used in a single game, were thrown into the affair by manager Burt Shotton—and two more were toiling rapidly in the bullpen in the final moments as the Brooks were striving to overcome the remaining four runs of their huge early deficit.

Not that the Yankees had any intention of ever letting the Brooks get close to even. They kept pouring it on against Banta in the fourth, when DiMaggio drove his towering smash deep into the lower seats just a foot inside the foul line; against Banta again in the fifth, when Woodling opened with a hot double to right and ultimately came home on Coleman's grounder to Hodges, who made a poor bouncing peg to the plate after having stepped on first for the out; and then against Carl Erskine in the sixth.

So the Brooks were behind, 10-1, at this point, when they finally decided it was time to avert what was fast becoming their worst Series licking of all time. They had been beaten, 8-1, by the Indians in 1920, and 10-3 by the Yankees in '47. This, though, figured to be the bloodiest thing in Brooklyn since Murder, Inc.

Were the Brooks discouraged? Not so that they'd stop trying to achieve the impossible. While Palica and Minner were muffling the Yank bats over the final three frames, the Brooks, it must be admitted, went down swinging spiritedly. They powdered Raschi out of action in the seventh, when, with one down, Jorgenson strolled and Snider buzzed him to third with a hit through the right side. Robinson's deep fly to left delivered Snider and then, after Hermanski also walked, Hodges hammered his three-run circuit far into the left seats.

Casey Stengel, the Yankee manager who played enough ball at Ebbets Field in his youth to appreciate the fact that the impossible can happen there, decided it was about time, with his lead gashed to 10-6, to start worrying. So he pulled Page from the pen and relaxed as Joe blazed three straight strikes past pinch-swinger Luis Olmo.

That was it. The Brooks were through scoring—but they weren't quite through threatening. In the eighth, Edwards banged a pinch-hit single through the left side, only to be doubled up on Reese's comeback smash to the box. Then Ed Miksis gave the crowd one last fleeting hope by opening the ninth with a pinch-hit cracker down the left line for two bases. But Page poured it on. Snider fanned . . . Robinson fanned . . . and, after Hermanski strolled, Hodges fanned.

It was over, and now the Yankees were doing the usual backslapping and joy-jumping as they rushed for the dugout—and the Brooks were doing the usual forlorn step that marks a loser. And the champagne flowed at the Yankees' Biltmore headquarters last night, just as it had flowed for victory toasts in 12 of the 16 Series in which they have been involved. While over in Brooklyn's HQ at the St. George, the boys settled for beer and such, and second-guessed the games far into the night, just as has been Brooklyn's fate in all four other futile attempts to become baseball champions of the world—in 1916, 1920, 1941, and 1947.

Their last three Series lickings have been by the Yankees, and they don't mind telling you it's getting downright monotonous. ■

A joyous Casey Stengel and his wife dance at a victory dinner after the 1949 World Series. Mrs. Stengel has recovered nicely from the heart attack she suffered during the Series. (News photo by Ebbs Breuer.)

Casey Goes to Bat—Gets Raises for Raschi, Yogi

by Joe Trimble

St. Petersburg—Casey Stengel quit being a mere sideline rooter for his holdout group this afternoon and took an active part in helping two of them win big increases. The manager made successful pleas to George Weiss on behalf of Yogi Berra and Vic Raschi and his eloquence settled all differences. Berra signed for about $19,000—a raise of $5,000—and Raschi settled for $30,000—a boost of $12,000.

Both players said that they had gotten good deals and were satisfied. Berra had been seeking $22,000 and Raschi, a 21-game winner, wanted $35,000. Vic felt that he ought to be worth as much as Joe Page and he pegged his future at the level upon which newspaper guessers had put Page's contract. Actually, Page is getting $32,500 . . . a number which makes him the highest-paid pitcher in Yank history.

Weiss admitted that it was Stengel who effected the compromises and George will be perfectly willing to listen to the manager's ideas about the paychecks which should go to the two remaining holdouts—Tom Byrne and Bobby Brown. Both will be asked to come to camp for talks soon.

WADDAYA SAY, UMP? The Phils' Dick Sisler looks up for a sign from Berry and gets it—OUT—on a pickoff by Mize at first. The Big Cat looks on in grim satisfaction after getting the peg from Berra in the sixth. Dick had just banged out his first hit of the 1950 World Series—a clutch single that scored Ennis to tie the game at 1-1. (News photo by Hank Olen.)

The Phils' hopes soared when Granny Hamner slid past Yogi Berra on Goliat's single to give the Whiz Kids a brief 2-1 lead late in the third game of the 1950 World Series. The Yankees won the game, 3-2, and went on to sweep the Phils in four straight to capture their 13th World Championship. (News photo by Hank Olen.)

Both Yogi and Vic are in very good shape and, after a few days of practice, will be as advanced as the others, who began training a week ago. They weren't able to get into uniform today because morning rain flooded the ball field. The entire squad was given the day off, Stengel being afraid to risk an injury in the soft ground. "Things are going too good this year," he explained. "Don't want to see those hospital charts this early."

The manager actually talked Berra into signing—after getting Weiss to raise his initial offer to $16,000. Berra has much more faith in Casey than in Weiss, who once paid him $90 a month as a rookie with Norfolk. That was in 1943, before the catcher went into the Navy. Each player also received a dollar a night for supper money then. Berra complained that it was not enough and one night he went on a sit-down strike, refusing to catch unless he received another dollar to ease his hunger pains. That worked, so he struck for a

raise. Healthy young ball players were scarce—he was just 18—and he won an increase to $140.

Raschi's late-season troubles were the basis for Weiss offering him less than the pitcher desired. Vic won 15 games by July 21 and then staggered all over the place trying to get the remaining six. He never complained about a thing, although forced to work with three days of rest between starts in the hottest part of the summer.

Stengel, in selling Weiss a bill of goods, took the blame for that today. "He had two things against him," Casey volunteered, "pitching shortages and Stengel. I didn't have enough pitchers to give him proper spacing between jobs. I knew he was tired and could have used a week's vacation, but in that kind of pennant race I couldn't take the pressure off him. One day, when he had a big lead against the White Sox, I took him out, figuring to win easy, so they tied it up and I had to go 13 innings and use up Page before winning." ■

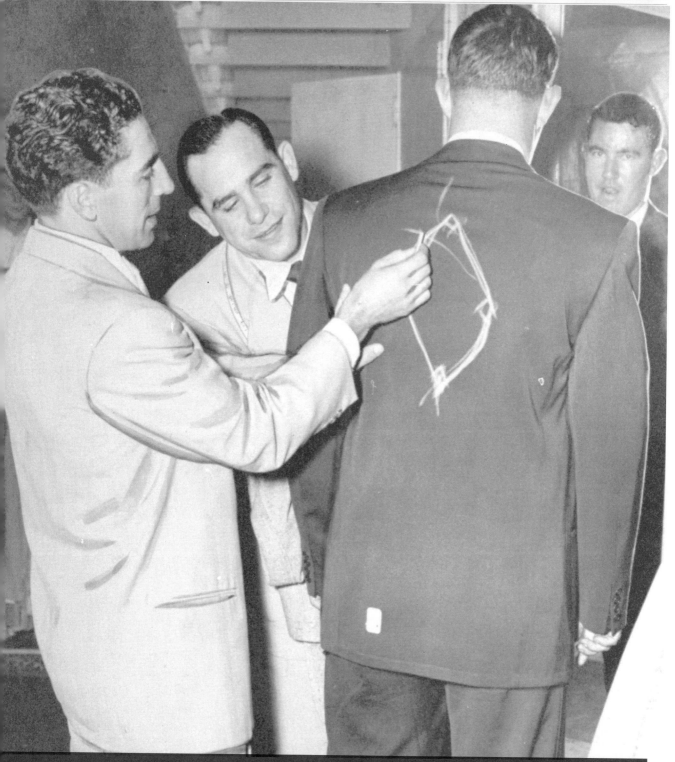

"During salary negotiations with Yankee GM George Weiss, Yogi predicted he would win the league's MVP. When Weiss countered that some of the papers were saying there were others more valuable, Yogi reportedly replied "I read only them papers which say I'm the most valuable."

2

1951: MVP

	G	AB	R	H	2B	3B	HR	RBI	BB	SB	BA	SA
1951:	141	547	92	161	19	4	27	88	44	5	.294	.492

Considered by many baseball experts the greatest player of the 1950s, Yogi won three MVP awards in the decade—the first in 1951. Yogi's reputation as the "toughest out" in baseball—along with his .294 batting average, 88 RBIs, 27 homers, and leadership behind the plate—helped him edge out St. Louis pitcher Ned Garver and teammate Allie Reynolds in one of the closest MVP races ever.

While Yogi's first MVP award was a special honor, it was only one of his many highlights in 1951. Yogi was behind the plate for both of Allie Reynolds' no-hitters—the second one ending in dramatic fashion with Ted Williams at the plate. The Yankees also captured their third straight World Series championship and, during the late-September pennant stretch, Yogi welcomed the birth of his second son, Tim.

Never one to let success go to his head, Yogi spent the off-season just as he always had— working. After the 1951 season, Yogi was schooled in the fine art of selling suits by fellow Yankee MVP Phil Rizzuto. ■

No two-headed monster this . . . it's only Yogi Berra and his happy mirror-self after he'd learned the result of the AL's MVP ballot. The Yank catcher, who's bound to hold his new honor over George Weiss' head at contract time, heard the news while instructing class at the American Baseball Academy in the 212th AAA Armory. (News photo by Arthur Buckley.)

November 9, 1951

Yogi, Garver, Allie 1-2-3 in MVP Vote

by Joe Trimble

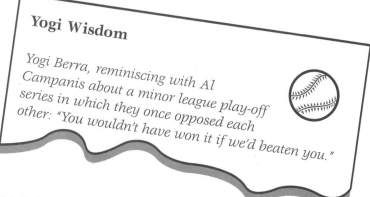

Yogi Wisdom

Yogi Berra, reminiscing with Al Campanis about a minor league play-off series in which they once opposed each other: "You wouldn't have won it if we'd beaten you."

Yogi Berra, the squat character who was labeled a "clown" when he became a Yankee regular in 1947, yesterday became the Most Valuable Player in the American League for 1951. The catcher just nosed out pitcher Ned Garver, the Browns' "one-man team," and Allie Reynolds, the Bombers' double no-hit right-hander, in one of the closest contests in the history of the award.

A committee of 24 members of the Baseball Writers Association of America—three voters from each of the league's eight cities—made the selections. Each scribe named ten men in order of preference, then added a list of players deserving "honorable mention."

BERRA POLLED 184 points, with Garver getting 157 and Reynolds 125. All three were named first on six ballots, but Berra gained his edge through second-, third-, and fourth-place designations. Yogi was named on 23 ballots, Garver on 20, and Reynolds on only 12. A first-place vote was worth 14 points, second nine, third eight, and so on, down to one for 10th.

Yogi Berra, Yankee catcher named the AL's MVP for the 1951 season, relaxes with his son, Larry, 2, and wife, Carmen, in their Woodcliff Lake, N.J., home. (News photo by Leonard Detrick.)

Warming up a two-year-old pitcher. (News photo by Leonard Detrick.)

Only three others received as many as 100 points. Orestes Minoso, the White Sox's brilliant rookie, was fourth with 120. He received one first-place nomination. Bob Feller, Indians' hurler who was not named first on any ballot, gained enough other designations to finish fifth with 118. Ferris Fain, first baseman of the A's and the league-leading hitter with a .344 mark, gained 103 and was named at the top of one ballot.

ELLIS KINDER, aged-in-the-wood Red Sox relief pitcher, finished seventh with 66 points and was named first by two selectors. Yanks hurler Vic Raschi ran eighth with 64 points, though none for first place. Gil McDougald, the champs' rookie infielder, was ninth with 63, and Bobby Avila, Tribe second baseman, completed the first ten with 49. Neither Mac nor Avila received a first-place vote. Phil Rizzuto and Ed Lopat, each of whom drew one first-place vote, finished 11th and 12th, so six of the first dozen positions went to the Yanks.

Yogi led the Bombers in slugging with 88 RBIs and 27 homers, but tailed off near the end of the season and finished with a .294 BA in 141 games. "I was afraid I had blown it with the bad finish," the 26-year-old catcher said yesterday. "I was pretty sure Reynolds would be picked, especially after the no-hitters."

THE VOTES WERE counted in the Radio City office of Commissioner Ford Frick Wednesday afternoon and Berra first learned of the honor when a photographer sought him while Yogi was conducting a

AL's Top Players Over the Years

1951-YOGI BERRA	1936-Lou Gehrig
1950-Phil Rizzuto	1935-H. Greenburg
1949-Ted Williams	1934-Mickey Cochrane
1948-Lou Boudreau	1933-Jimmie Foxx
1947-Joe DiMaggio	1932-Jimmie Foxx
1946-Ted Williams	1931-Lefty Grove
1945-Hal Newhouser	1930-No selection
1944-Hal Newhouser	1929-No selection
1943-Spud Chandler	1928-Mickey Cochrane
1942-Joe Gordon	1927-Lou Gehrig
1941-Joe DiMaggio	1926-George Burns
1940-H. Greenburg	1925-R. Peckinpaugh
1939-Joe DiMaggio	1924-Walter Johnson
1938-Jimmie Foxx	1923-Babe Ruth
1937-C. Gehringer	1922-George Sisler

TOPS IN AL

(First-place vote in parentheses)

Player, Club	Pts.
1. Yogi Berra, New York (6)	184
2. Ned Garver, St. Louis (6)	157
3. Allie Reynolds, New York (6)	125
4. Orestes Minoso, Chicago (1)	120
5. Bob Feller, Cleveland	118
6. Ferris Fain, Philadelphia (1)	103
7. Ellis Kinder, Boston (2)	66
8. Vic Raschi, New York	64
9. Gil McDougald, New York	63
10. Bobby Avila, Cleveland	49
11. Phil Rizzuto, New York (1)	47
12. Ed Lopat, New York (1)	44
13. Ted Williams, Boston	35
14. Eddie Joost, Philadelphia	32
15. George Kell, Detroit	30
16. Early Wynn, Cleveland	29
17. Nelson Fox, Chicago	25
18. Billy Goodman, Boston	21
19. Dom DiMaggio, Boston	16
20. Gus Zernial, Philadelphia	15

class at the American Baseball Academy in the 212th AAA Armory at 62d St. and Columbus Ave., Manhattan.

Yogi had a date with his wife, Carmen, in the evening for dinner and the hockey game at the Garden. He met her at a restaurant and said, "I've got good news for you."

SHE THOUGHT IT was about some household furnishings they had been unable to find in the stores and wasn't impressed when Yogi told her of the MVP award.

"I didn't realize what a big thing it is until other people came over and talked with us," Carmen said. "Then I caught on and we ordered some champagne to celebrate."

Yogi described the news as one of the biggest thrills of his life. "It's great to be classed with fellows like DiMaggio and Rizzuto who have won the award," he pointed out. "I sure hope I can win it a couple of more times, like Joe did."

DiMAG, INCIDENTALLY, failed to get a single point for the first time in his career. Ted Williams fared poorly, too. The Sox slugger finished 13th with 35 points, none from a first-place nomination.

Berra is only the second catcher to win the AL prize, Mickey Cochrane having gained it twice. A catcher also won this year in the NL, Roy Campanella of the Dodgers.

The award means an additional talking point in Yogi's annual salary battle with George Weiss, the Yankee general manager. The catcher took down about $27,000 last year and is certain to scream for 40 grand next year.

"KNOWING WEISS," Yogi said, with a grin, "I'll be lucky if he doesn't try to cut my salary." ∎

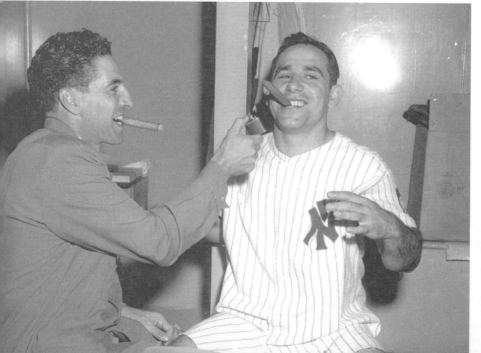

INDULGENT POP. Yogi Berra, who's been passing out cigars in honor of his 2nd son, indulges in one himself with Phil Rizzuto (l.) in the Yanks' dressing room. (News photo by Seymour Wally.)

Yogi flashes his famous MVP smile.

September 29, 1951

Reynolds' No-Hitter Won Twice

Yankees 8, Red Sox 0

by Joe Trimble

The Yankees added to their fabled, glorious history yesterday at the Stadium by winning their 18th pennant—and they did it with a flourish that even the famed New York clubs of the past never achieved. The Bombers carried Casey Stengel to his third straight flag by beating the Red Sox in a climactic double bill—winning the opening game on a no-hitter.

Allie Reynolds became the first pitcher in the history of the American League to hurl two no-hit, no-run games in one season as he zeroed the Hose in the first game, 8-0, despite some tense moments on the final out. Vic Raschi, the team's other strong right arm, fired the 11-3 nightcap victory which clinched the pennant.

Stengel has now won three pennants in his first three years at the helm, matching the records set early in the century by Frank

YANKEES 8, RED SOX 0

RED SOX

	ab	r	h	bi
DiMaggio, cf	2	0	0	0
Pesky, 2b	4	0	0	0
Williams, lf	3	0	0	0
Vollmer, rf	2	0	0	0
Goodman, 1b	3	0	0	0
Boudreau, ss	3	0	0	0
Hatfield, 3b	3	0	0	0
Robinson, c	3	0	0	0
Parnell, p	1	0	0	0
Scarbo'gh, p	1	0	0	0
Taylor, p	0	0	0	0
a-Maxwell	1	0	0	0
Totals	**26**	**0**	**0**	**0**

YANKEES

	ab	r	h	bi
Rizzuto, ss	5	1	1	0
Coleman, 2b	3	2	1	1
Bauer, lf	4	0	1	1
DiMaggio, cf	4	0	1	0
McDougald, 3b	3	1	1	1
Berra, c	4	0	1	1
Woodling, lf	4	2	2	1
Collins, 1b	4	2	2	2
Reynolds, p	3	0	0	0
Totals	**34**	**8**	**10**	**7**

Red Sox	000	000	000	—0
Yankees	202	102	010	—8

a-Grounded out for Taylor in 9th.
LOB-Red Sox 3, Yankees 5. 2B-Collins.
HR-Woodling, Collins. SB-Coleman.
S-Reynolds. DP-Red Sox 1, Yanks 1.

	IP	H	R	ER	BB	SO
Parnell (L, 18-10)	4	5	4	4	2	2
Scarborough	2	3	3	3	0	0
Taylor	2	2	1	0	0	0
Reynolds (W, 17-8)	9	0	0	0	4	9

T-2:33. A-39,038.

Allie Reynolds cele-brates after he no-hitted the Red Sox at the Stadium, 8-0, to become the first pitcher in American League history to hurl two classics in one season. Woodling, Berra, and Collins (l. to r.) sur-round Reynolds. (News photo by Hank Olen.)

Chance and Hughie Jennings. Chance led the Cubs to the top in 1906-'07-'08 as a new boss, and Jennings matched him with the Tigers in 1907-'08-'09.

Dramatic ninth

This was the 92nd no-hitter since the two leagues began in 1900 but probably the first one in which the hurler had to get the 27th out TWICE. The drama, always great as a pitcher tries for a no-hit game, was heightened as the ninth began with Charley Maxwell, a pinch hitter. Maxwell fouled off half a dozen pitches, then grounded to second base. Dom DiMaggio then drew a walk. Johnny Pesky, a dangerous poke hitter, came up and took a called third strike, a sharp curve.

The crowd screamed wildly in a swelling roar as the next batter stepped up. Reynolds was down to the final out, and no less than Ted Williams, the greatest hitter in the league, was at bat. Reynolds was going to have to earn this prize. Ted took a half-speed pitch for a strike. Reynolds then fired a fastball which Ted fouled high in the air about 15 feet behind home plate. Yogi Berra settled under it and then staggered around as the ball descended. He misjudged it and Reynolds, seeing this, rushed up to try to grab the ball or maybe catch the carom off the catcher's mitt. But Allie arrived too late as Yogi sprawled in the red clay and let the ball tip off his glove.

The pitcher, who could have been pardoned for slugging Yogi, carefully picked the squat man up, patted him on the fanny, and threw an arm around his shoulders—like a father comforting a small, unhappy boy. Allie then resumed his place on the mound and slammed another fastball to the plate. Ted skyrocketed this one, too, over in the vicinity of the Yankee dugout.

The noncompeting players scattered. Yogi came over and this time, on a far more difficult play, made the catch and squeezed the ball to be sure. ∎

Yogi Berra misses a Ted Williams pop-up in the ninth inning with two outs and a no-hitter on the line. (News photo by Hank Olen.)

Yanks Clinch, 4-3, as Giant Rally Fails

Bauer Triple Payoff; His Catch Ends It

by Joe Trimble

The strong and enduring Yanks dynasty stood firm against the miracle Giants, stonily turned the fabulous NL club's drive toward still another storybook climax yesterday, and so the longest baseball season in history finally came to a close. The Jints, trailing by three runs in the ninth, loaded the bases with none out and just missed pulling another of their fantastic finishes as they went down, 4-3, at the Stadium.

The Series victory, four games to two, earned the Bombers their 14th world championship in 18 years and their third in succession under the laughing leadership of Casey Stengel. The funny old man, nicest millionaire to be found anywhere, established a personal record of achievement by leading the team to the top in his first three years as manager.

The Giants, whose miraculous road to victory in the NL turned out to be the most amazing baseball story of all time, simply waited too long yesterday.

They threw away many early opportunities and finally time ran out on them when it seemed to the 61,711 spectators that they might yet create another miracle. The game ended with Hank Bauer, the rugged Yankee right fielder, clutching a line drive while skidding along the seat of his pants.

That Bauer should catch the final out in his strong hands was rather fitting and made for a nice ending for the Yankee fans. For it was the broad-backed ex-Marine who had slugged the Yanks to the top.

Hank, who stopped enough shrapnel at Iwo Jima to win a Purple Heart, had crashed the winning hit in the sixth inning, a 400-foot triple with the bases full, two out, and a 3-2 count on him. The long smash cleared the head of left fielder Monte Irvin, who was twisting and turning uncertainly on his muscle-torn left thigh as he rushed back for the ball.

That wallop broke a 1-1 tie and sealed the fate of Leo Durocher's Dandies of Destiny. ∎

Grateful Stengel Will Return in '52

October 11, 1951—Of the two big Yankee question marks for 1952, at least one was answered definitely in the winners' clubhouse after the Series clincher yesterday—manager Casey Stengel will be back. After emphasizing that he plans to return next spring to fulfill his contract, which still has another year to run, Casey elbowed through the crowd of scribes and fotogs to reach his "big man," Joe DiMaggio. Casey gave him a fatherly pat on the arm and said, "We couldn't have done it without you." It carried the silent but obvious postscript: "And I hope you change your mind about retiring, so you can help us do it again next year." Casey then proceeded to thank each player individually.

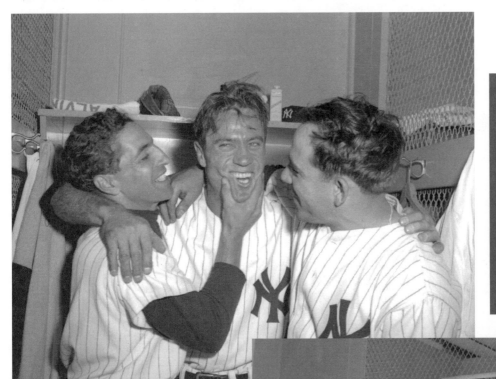

Phil Rizzuto (l.) Hank Bauer (c.) and Yogi Berra (r.) celebrate the Yankees' World Championship. It was Bauer's bases-loaded triple that put the Yanks ahead for good and his spectacular game-ending catch that sealed the victory. (News photo by Ed Clarity.)

Yankee Clipper Joe DiMaggio rubs Yogi's head after the Yanks' victory over the Dodgers. Yogi got two hits and Joe one in the World Series clincher. (News photo by Tom Watson.)

Seconds after the Yankees won yesterday's game and the Series, they rushed jubilantly off the Stadium diamond, led by coach Jim Turner (l.). Among others are starting pitcher Raschi (in jacket) and McDougald (over Raschi's shoulder), congratulating pitcher Kuzava, who finished the game, and pitcher Sain (hand at waist), who relieved Raschi. (News photo by Ed Clarity.)

"A nickel ain't worth a dime anymore."

3
1952-53: Anchoring a Dynasty

	G	AB	R	H	2B	3B	HR	RBI	BB	SB	BA	SA
1952:	142	534	97	146	17	1	30	98	66	2	.273	.478
1953:	137	503	80	149	23	5	27	108	50	0	.296	.523

In contrast to the long-term, multimillion-dollar contracts that dominate baseball today, one-year contracts were the order of the day in the 1950s. The annual negotiations and signings of star players like Yogi often made for great theater, with pay cuts being reported as often as raises.

Yogi's engaging, lighthearted demeanor belied the fact that when it came time for contract negotiations, he never shied away from a confrontation with Yankee GM George Weiss. More than once in his career, Yogi even went as far as staging his own holdout to ensure that he received his due.

Fresh off his MVP season, however, no holdout was necessary. Yogi signed quickly for a hefty $7,000 raise and was promptly installed as Joe DiMaggio's successor in the cleanup spot. Despite his objections to batting fourth, Yogi came through with a record-setting year, and the Yankees maintained their dominance with victories in the 1952 and 1953 World Series. ■

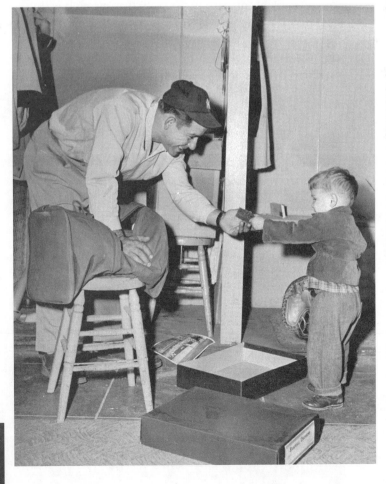

Larry Berra, 2$^{1}/_{2}$, gets Pop to lay off the comics long enough to give him a few tips on catching as Yogi picks up his equipment at the Stadium.
(News photo by Ossie LeViness.)

January 24, 1952

Yogi Signs for 35Gs

by Joe Trimble

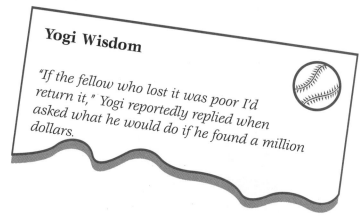

Yogi Wisdom

"If the fellow who lost it was poor I'd return it," Yogi reportedly replied when asked what he would do if he found a million dollars.

Yogi Berra and Gil McDougald, the Yanks' prize-winning pair, came into the club offices yesterday to formally accept some of the $90,000 that the club will not have to pay Joe DiMaggio this year. Berra, the AL's Most Valuable Player, signed a contract for $35,000 and McDougald, Rookie of the Year, picked a pact calling for $12,000—a raise of nearly 100%.

Berra received $28,000 last year, so he gets a raise of seven grand. Mac worked under a $5,000 rookie minimum last season until he made the team, then was raised to $6,500.

"I received the second contract after May 15, when the squad was cut to 25 players," he said. "It called for a raise over the first one and the one I signed today is almost double that. It's as close to a 100% better as you can get."

Yogi said he was completely satisfied, which is quite a novelty because the catcher never before has been in the fold this early. Last year he missed the first ten days of spring training while waging a holdout duel.

"I got what I wanted," the character insisted, grinning. "I just told George Weiss the facts and we agreed."

A good portion of yesterday's pre-game ceremonies was taken up by passing out awards to members of the World Champs, and manager Casey Stengel was beaming all over the park. (L. to r.) Yogi Berra, the K.M. Landis Memorial as the league's MVP; Allie Reynolds, N.Y. Newspaper Guild's Page 1 Award; Stengel; Phil Rizzuto, the Babe Ruth Memorial Award; and Gil McDougald, Rookie of the Year. (News photo by Hank Olen.)

Everything is peaches and cream between Yogi Berra and Yank "write"-hand man Roy Hamey as the Bomber backstop signs his new pact for $35,000. But hurler Allie Reynolds isn't having any of what Roy offered as he stuffs his contract back in his pocket. He's looking for a boost from last year's $35,000. (News photo by Pete Watson.)

Weiss was present during the interview and laughed.

"Yogi told me some facts and I told him some others," he said. "Neither his facts nor figures were the same as mine, but we were close enough to work it out."

The general manager was referring to the fact that Berra slumped badly in the last month of the season and made the winning of the flag more difficult than it should have been. In the first five months, he was the strong man of the club, bearing the load which a faltering DiMag simply couldn't handle.

The relief from Joe's big salary gives Weiss an opportunity to be a bit more openhanded than usual. Therefore, there seems to be little chance of holdouts. Vic Raschi, when his contract is announced, will be second-highest man on the list, at about $40,000.

WITH BERRA happy, and Raschi and Allie Reynolds due to be well taken care of, the only star who has not yet been signed or announced as satisfied is Phil Rizzuto.

The Scooter will sign in time for $45,000. Although the club has given raises almost universally, the payroll will not be as high as it was last year. ∎

Yogi on Sleeping

"I usually take a two-hour nap from one to four."

"If I didn't wake up I'd still be sleeping."

"I had to get up to answer the phone anyway," Yogi replied when a caller apologized for waking him.

March 7, 1952

Berra Inherits Joe's Old Cleanup Spot

by Joe Trimble

Manager Casey Stengel today nominated Yogi Berra as cleanup hitter of the Yankees and hopes that the young man will take kindly to his new duties. In the past, when Joe DiMaggio was still around, Berra batted fourth under protest.

He didn't care to fill in for The Clipper and cared less about shouldering the responsibility of the star role in the batting order.

Stengel revealed his choice for the job this afternoon, when he wrote out the lineup for the opening exhibition against the Cardinals here Saturday. Casey, always one to take the bull by the horns, simply announced that the catcher would bat fourth. There will be no change or switch, regardless of the type of opposing pitcher, unless Yogi shows his old reluctance to tackle the big job.

"I don't wanna bat fourth," Berra told Casey last September, when it became necessary to drop DiMaggio out of the cleanup spot. "I can't hit no good there. I dunno what happens. I tighten up, and I ain't no good. Let me bat lower down. I like it fifth."

Casey, hard-pressed to keep the club from toppling out of first place at the time, shrugged off Yogi's protest. But Berra went into a tailspin as cleanup hitter and became almost useless with the bat. Stengel was compelled to revise the lineup. He used Mize, Woodling, Bauer and even Joe Collins at times before reinstating DiMaggio for the final two weeks of the season.

Should Yogi again get the "willies" and fail to flog the ball as cleanup man, filling DiMag's batting spot could become a year-long problem. Offhand, there's no other man on the club qualified for the job.

Berra plays every day. He led the club in RBIs with 88 and homers with 27. He is the best long-ball hitter on the club.■

BERRA SETS AL HR MARK FOR CATCHERS

by Joe Trimble

September 29, 1952—The Yankees closed the AL season this afternoon when they took a 9-4 trouncing from the Athletics. The game was important only in that it served as the framework for another record-breaking batting performance by one of the Bombers.

Yogi Berra belted his 30th homer to establish a new AL mark for catchers, surpassing the previous high of 29, which Bill Dickey set in 1937.

Ferris Fain rapped a triple in the sixth inning, when the A's scored eight runs off lefty Bill Miller. Although that was his only hit, it helped the A's first sacker to repeat as batting champion of the league with a mark of .327. He is the sixth man to lead the loop in successive seasons. Fain batted .344 in 1951.

Mickey Mantle played the entire game, getting one single in four times at bat. This enabled him to tie Gene Woodling for top average among the champions, each finishing with .311. Woodling didn't play, due to a groin injury. Mickey's average was a mite better than Gene's if carried out a fifth decimal point, .31104 to .31103.

A crowd of 11,893 came out for the finale in gorgeous weather. The A's, by winning, clinched fourth place. This was only the second time they've finished in the first division since 1933. They also landed

MOST VALUABLE PLAYERS GET TOGETHER FROM THE LAST THREE YEARS. Yogi Berra, (with measuring tape), the 1951 MVP, Phil Rizzuto, (taking order for suit), 1950 MVP, and Bobby Shantz, (being fitted for suit), 1952 MVP.

New York Yankees Team 1953. Front row (sitting): Joseph Carrieri, Dick Manzidelis, batboys. Second row (l. to r.): Art Shallock, Ed Ford, Billy Martin, Phil Rizzuto, Larry Berra, Steve Kraly, Frank Crosetti (coach), Manager Casey Stengel, Jim Turner (coach), Gil McDougald, Irv Noren, Gene Woodling, Charley Silvera. Third row (l. to r.): Trainer Gus Mauch, Jim McDonald, Willie Miranda, Jerry Coleman, Bob Kuzava, Bill Miller, Tom Gorman, Bill Renna, Gus Triandos, Vic Raschi. Last row (l. to r.): Johnny Mize, Ed Lopat, Andy Carey, Mickey Mantle, Hank Bauer, Ralph Houk (coach), Johnny Sain, Don Bollweg, Allie Reynolds, Joe Collins.

Yanks Win Record 5th

Martin's Hit in 9th Clinches It, 4-3

by Joe Trimble

The Dodgers are dead, but they died like champions in the chill and gloom of the Stadium yesterday. The Yankees clapped the lid on the coffin—frustrating Brooklyn's seventh try for a World Championship. And dancing gleefully on the bier was impetuous Billy Martin, the fresh kid who is at once Casey Stengel's pride and problem child. The brash youngster exploded his 12th Series hit in the ninth inning to drive in the winning run of a sensational 4-3 victory which brought Stengel and his Bombers an unprecedented fifth straight world title.

Martin, who never stopped haunting the Brooks once in the six games, picked out a fastball by reliever Clem Labine and singled cleanly through the middle of the diamond to score Hank Bauer from second base. The Yankees, throwing off their reserve, bounced screaming from the dugout and mobbed the big-beaked kid who, more than anyone else, brought them the title and some $8,200 apiece in the lushest classic of all time.

It went into the ninth, with the Yanks leading 3-1, and the greatest team in Dodger history looked pretty sad. It looked like curtains when Gil Hodges hit a soft fly for the first out of the ninth.

There was a buzz of anticipation as Duke Snider stepped up. The big left swinger had been miserable in fanning three times against starter Whitey Ford, but now he had a crack at a right-hander.

Joe DiMaggio, considered the greatest center fielder in Yankee history, makes his appearance with his successor, Mickey Mantle. Joe gave the Mick the benefit of his knowledge as a hitter and fielder. Now it's up to Mickey.

Allie Reynolds got a 2-2 count on the Duke, then fired a knee-high fastball which seemed to go right over the plate. Snider froze as he took the pitch, then he cut a sigh of relief as umpire Bill Stewart called it a ball. Catcher Yogi Berra, Reynolds, and half the Yankee bench-warmers leaped high in disgust.

"No, no," screamed Berra. "Ya missed it, Bill, ya missed it!"

The NL umpire stood his ground and Reynolds resumed his job. Duke fouled off a couple and finally walked on a 3-2 pitch which was inside.

Furillo was next and now Reynolds was really firing. After going to 2-2, Carl stroked an outside pitch for a long drive which was foul by about 30 feet in the right-field stands. It was obvious that he was shooting in that direction, trying to drive the ball down the shortest possible route to the stands. The next pitch was high and the following one went right down the Burma Road, dropping into the seats about 310 feet from the plate.

As the ball soared in its flight, Bauer went back to the wall. He lunged against it, pushing furiously with his spikes in the ground and his shoulder against the three-foot-high fence, as if hoping some way to plunge through it and into the stands for the ball.

The Stadium roared in the wildest moment of the Series, the lights went on again in Brooklyn and Dodger bench-warmers streamed out to shake the hand of the man who had brought them from the jaws of death. Snider and Furillo circled the bases slowly, Carl basking in the reception. He had a right to same, for he had been more or less the batting bust of the Series and had hit into three double plays.

Reynolds, ashamed of himself, turned on the heat and whiffed Billy Cox and Labine to end the inning. The strikeout of his pitching opponent was Allie's 62nd in six Series, breaking Ruffing's former high of 61 in seven classics.

Now it was up to Labine, the young right-hander who had blossomed out as the Brooks' bullpen ace in the second half of the season. The crew-cut kid opened by walking Bauer on a 3-2 pitch which was high. Now the Yankee fans began to shout for the kill. Berra tried hard for the homer, but succeeded only in driving a sinking liner to Furillo.

Up came Mickey Mantle, the long-ball hitter of the Series, and he, too, was going for the fence.

Instead, he topped a sleazy little roller to the third base side of the mound. It was unplayable and went for a hit.

This stroke of luck moved Bauer to second and, with no base open, Labine had to pitch to Martin, the hero of the World Series by a mile. Billy, who earlier had made a double and who had been deprived of another hit by a tough scoring decision, took the first pitch, a ball. The next one was fast and low and he hacked it hard on the ground through the box. Bauer stormed home from second as Snider forlornly trotted in and fielded the ball.

Do you think any of us will live long enough to see Brooklyn win one of these things? ■

SERIES: GAME BY GAME ■
1953

FINAL STANDINGS

	W.	L.	Pct.
Yanks	4	2	.667
Dodgers	2	4	.333

First Game, Stadium, Sept. 30

	R	H	E
Dodgers	5	12	2
Yanks	9	12	0

Erskine, Hughes (2); LABINE (6), Wade (7) and Campanella; Reynolds, SAIN (6) and Berra.

Second Game, Stadium, Oct. 1

Dodgers	2	9	1
Yanks	4	5	0

ROE and Campanella; LOPAT and Berra

Third Game, Ebbets Field, Oct. 2

Yanks	2	6	0
Dodgers	3	9	0

RASCHI and Berra; ERSKINE and Campanella

Fourth Game, Ebbets Field, Oct. 3

Yanks	3	9	0
Dodgers	7	12	0

FORD, Gorman (2), Sain (5), Shallock (7) and Berra; LOES, Labine (9) and Campanella.

Fifth Game, Ebbets Field, Oct. 4

Yanks	11	11	1
Dodgers	7	14	1

MCDONALD, Kuzava (8), Reynolds (9) and Berra; PODRES, Meyer (3), Wade (8), Black (9) and Campanella

Sixth Game, Stadium, Oct. 5

Dodgers	3	8	3
Yanks	4	13	0

Erskine, Milliken (5), LABINE (7) and Campanella. Ford, REYNOLDS (8) and Berra.

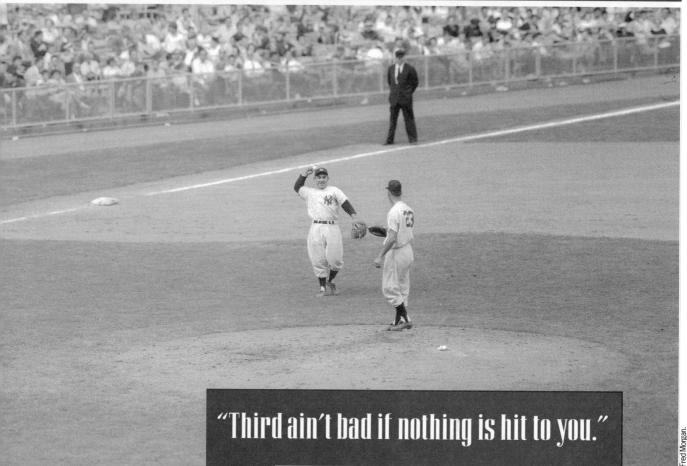

"Third ain't bad if nothing is hit to you."

News photo by Fred Morgan.

4

1954-55: It's Deja Vu All Over Again

	G	AB	R	H	2B	3B	HR	RBI	BB	SB	BA	SA
1954:	151	584	88	179	28	6	22	125	56	0	.307	.488
1955:	147	541	84	147	20	3	27	108	60	1	.272	.470

Narrow victories in the MVP voting were becoming Yogi's trademark. After his close win in 1951, Yogi again captured MVP honors by the slimmest of margins in 1954 and 1955. Commenting on Yogi's prowess in such close races, Daily News *sportswriter Dick Young speculated, only partly in jest, that it might just be because "Yogi is such a helluva guy."*

Whatever the margin, Yogi's three MVP trophies put him in select company with baseball's only other three-time winners: Joe DiMaggio, Jimmie Foxx, Stan Musial, and Roy Campanella, who also won his third MVP in 1955. Since that time, only two other players have earned three-time MVP honors — Yogi's teammate Mickey Mantle (1956, '57, '62) and Philadelphia's Mike Schmidt (1980, '81, '86).

Although the Yankees' string of five straight World Series appearances ended when Cleveland won the American League pennant in 1954, the Yankees returned to the fall classic in 1955 against the Brooklyn Dodgers. In a grueling seven-game series, the Dodgers finally captured the Championship with a 2-0 victory in the final game.

One of the enduring images of the 1955 series is the controversy surrounding Jackie Robinson's steal of home in Game 1. The debate over whether Robinson was safe raged to the point that the editorial page of the Daily News *weighed in with its opinion. Concluding that Yogi had committed interference on the play, the* Daily News *opined that Robinson was safe even if — as the photos show — his slide didn't beat Yogi's tag.* ∎

INCLUDING TIPS, YOGI'S DOING JUST FINE. White Sox catcher Sherman Lollar waits for a foul tip that seems to be glued to Yogi's bat. (News photo by Charles Hoff.)

December 10, 1954

Yogi Tops Three Indians for MVP Award

by Dick Young

In the closest election since the race for New York's governorship, Yogi Berra yesterday was named MVP of the American League. There will be no recount, but there will be plenty of howls inasmuch as Berra conquered through the division of the Cleveland vote among Larry Doby, Bobby Avila, and Bob Lemon. The chunky Yankee catcher, who also won the award in '51, compiled a point total of 230. Then came Doby with 210; Avila, 203; Minnie Minoso of the Chisox, 186; and Lemon, 179.

There will be no criticism of Yogi, whose value to the Yankees is unquestioned. Rather, there will be strong criticism of the system which repeatedly permits the divide-and-conquer result. Berra was a Yankee stickout. He received negligible competition from his mates. You must go down the list to 11th place before finding another Yankee—Bob Grim—who collected only 25 points.

Contrast that to the fact that the Indians placed three men among the first five, with a composite total of 592 points. Of the first-place votes, Yogi received 7. The three Clevelanders divided 15—five apiece. The remaining two first-place designations went to Minoso.

The voting is cast by a 24-man committee from the Baseball Writers' Association of America. It is an equitable board in that three men represent each AL city. Each voter names his 10 player choices in order, and the points are computed by awarding 15 for first place, nine for second, and then down the line, 8-7-6-5-4-3-2-1.

Berra, whose ability is surpassed only by his graciousness, received news of his election with embarrassed joy. "I'm very happy and very surprised," he said. "Those are some pretty good guys I beat out for it. I knew I was being considered but I didn't think I'd get it."

Yogi Berra, who for the second time in his career won the American League's Most Valuable Player award, is shown at Madison Square Garden, where he watched the doubleheader college games. He holds a basketball in his hand instead of the familiar baseball. (News photo by Charles Hoff).

Berra's powerful and consistent play throughout the season was responsible, almost exclusively, for his team's strong bid for its sixth straight AL flag. Even though the Yanks failed to stop Cleveland, Yogi kept them in contention. He missed only five games behind the plate and in two of those he pinch-hit. He wound up with a .307 average, banged 22 homers, and his 125 RBIs fell one short of Doby's league high.

While no Yankee compared with Yogi, the competition among the Indians clearly explains the split voting. Doby was RBI champ. Avila won the batting crown at .341. And Lemon was top pitcher with a 23-and-7 record.

It is interesting to note that when Yogi won in '51, the reverse situation existed. He edged out Ned Garver of the Brownies that year in spite of strong competition from his teammate Allie Reynolds. Each of the three received six first-place votes.

Rarely does a catcher make MVP. In the 33 years of the award, the only other backstop to win was Mickey Cochrane and he, like Yogi, did it twice, in 1928 and 1934. There have been six repeaters, including Yankees Lou Gehrig and Joe DiMaggio. Gehrig took it in '27 and '30. DiMag was a three-timer—'39, '41 and '47. The immortal Babe Ruth was named only once, in 1923. This year is the 11th of 33 that a Yankee has won.

There have been other cases of a split vote that created widespread comment. In recent years, Bob Elliott, 1947, and Hank Sauer, 1952, topped the NL award due to widely divided votes to Dodger contenders.

At the other extreme, last year's AL winner, Al Rosen, was a unanimous choice of the 24-man board. The man who finished second to Rosen was Berra.

The designation of MVP usually means additional money in the paycheck—but not this time. Yogi signed his 1955 contract a month ago—the first Yankee to agree.

"Some people told me I should have waited for just this reason," Yogi said yesterday, "but I'm satisfied. They treated me real good."

He has come a long way in eight seasons, this 29-year-old lovable character who laughs off the barbs about his anthropoidal appearance. When he joined the Yankees in '47 he made $5,000. Next year, he will make ten times that. ■

Glad for Yogi

Larry Doby, runner-up to Yogi Berra in the MVP balloting, said yesterday:

"I'm a little disappointed. I thought I might get it. But I'm glad for Yogi. He's one swell guy and a great ball player. I'd like to express my appreciation to all the fellows who voted for me."

1954 MVP runner-up Larry Doby.

December 4, 1955

Third MVP for Yanks' Berra

by Dick Young

Yogi Berra today joined Joe DiMaggio, Jimmie Foxx, and Stan Musial as the only three-time winners of the Most Valuable Player Award. The stumpy Yankee backstop was named the stickout player of the AL for 1955 in one of the closest, and perhaps one of the strangest, voting contests in the 25-year history of the award.

Berra compiled 218 points on the basis of the system employed by the Baseball Writers Association of America, which awards 14 points for a first-place vote, nine for a second, eight for a third, and so on down to one point for 10th. The election committee, as always, was composed of 24 members, three from each AL franchise city.

Second was Al Kaline, Detroit's fine young outfielder, with 201—a photo ahead of the 200 compiled by Al Smith, Cleveland's valuable outfielder–third sacker. Then came the big gap to fourth place, where Ted Williams finished with 143. Mickey Mantle was fifth at 113.

The incongruity of the voting for the first three men is the oddest feature of the election. Berra received seven first-place votes. Kaline, the league's batting champ, pulled only four. But Smith, who wound up in third place, matched Yogi's seven. What's more, Smith drew five second-place votes to only two for Berra.

That gave Smith a strong lead in the first two voting columns, but then Yogi made his move. He received six third-place mentions. Smith didn't get one. That's where Yogi wrapped it up—on those third-place votes valued at eight points per. Kaline had six seconds and three thirds and six fourth-place votes.

Other oddities:

One writer ignored Smith completely, rating 10 others ahead of him. Only Berra and Kaline were named on all 24 ballots.

Yankee catcher Yogi Berra grins over his 1955 contract in the club office. He signed up to the tune of $48,000, making him the highest-paid catcher in baseball history. (News photo by Bob Koller.)

Ted Williams received just one first-place vote, and was unnamed on four tickets.

Mickey Mantle rated high without the aid of a first-place vote.

Gil McDougald, who had Casey Stengel as a gratuitous campaign manager, pulled two firsts, then was mentioned by only one other writer, who tossed the Yankee infielder a fifth.

Statistically, Berra did not have one of his better years. His .272 batting average was well below his lifetime figure of .293. But Yogi's hits drove in runs and won games, and when a player wins them for a pennant club, he inevitably has a "Most Valuable" edge on his competition.

Here's how Yogi's 1955 figures stack up against his competitors:

	G	BA	HR	RBI
Berra	147	.272	27	108
Kaline	152	.340	27	102
Smith	154	.306	22	77
Williams	98	.356	28	83

The only explanation of the MVP vote, then, would seem to be that the committee members reasoned that Kaline, for all his value to the Detroit club, could not lift it above fifth place; that Smith fizzled toward the end, and so did Cleveland; that Williams, as great as he is, could not raise the Bosox any higher than fourth after pumping them up from seventh when he returned from "retirement" in May.

Or maybe it's just that Yogi is such a helluva guy.

Berra first won MVP in '51, when he beat out Ned Garver, 184-157. He copped again last year, topping Larry Doby, 230-210. By repeating this time, Yogi becomes the first Yankee to repeat on successive years. Jimmie Foxx did it with the A's in '32-'33; Hal Newhouser with the Tigers in '44-'45.

Foxx also won in '38 to become the first three-timer. Joe DiMaggio's three awards were well spaced, in '39, '41, '47. Stan Musial, only three-time winner in the NL, racked them up in '43, '46, '48.

Berra, now 30 and presumably at the peak of his career, could go on to become the first four-timer. When contacted at his home in Woodcliff Lake, N.J., Yogi expressed his genuine elation by saying: "No matter how many times you win it, it's always a thrill. I'm gonna try and win it again." ■

MVP Vote Getters

	Player	Club	Pts.
1.	Larry Berra	New York	218
2.	Al Kaline	Detroit	201
3.	Alphone Smith	Cleveland	200
4.	Ted Williams	Boston	143
5.	Mickey Mantle	New York	113
6.	Ray Narlesk	Cleveland	90
7.	Nelson Fox	Chicago	84
8.	Hank Bauer	New York	64
9.	Vic Power	Kansas City	55
10.	Jackie Jensen	Boston	39
11.	Sherman Lollar	Chicago	37
12.	Gil McDougald	New York	34
13.	Bill Klaus	Boston	27
14.	Tommy Byrne	New York	24
15.	Whitey Ford	New York	21
16.	Ray Boone	Detroit	16
17.	Roy Sievers	Washington	9
18.	Harvey Kuenn	Detroit	8
19.	Billy Pierce	Chicago	8
20.	Dave Philley	Cleveland-Baltimore	6
21.	Early Wynn	Cleveland	6
22.	Elmer Valo	Kansas City	5
23.	Mickey Vernon	Washington	4
24.	Billy Hoeft	Detroit	1
25.	Don Mossi	Cleveland	1
26.	Frank Sullivan	Boston	1

Dodgers Champs! Podres Wins, 2-0

Johnny Brilliant in Second World Series Victory

by Joe Trimble

They won't make Oct. 4 a red-letter day in Brooklyn. They'll print it in letters of gold from now on because it's only the greatest date in the history of the batty borough—the day those darling Dodgers finally won the World Series. At exactly 3:45 yesterday afternoon at the Stadium, the Brooks got the third out of a 2-0 victory over the Yankees in the seventh and deciding game.

What kind of a date has it been? Well, on Oct. 4, 1861, the Union forces massed to form the Army of the Potomac; in 1864, the Erie Railroad opened (probably not on time); in 1940, Hitler and Mussolini met at the Brenner Pass; and in 1944, the U.S. Army broke through the German West Wall. Al Smith, the beloved Governor of New York and Presidential candidate, also died on the latter date.

As far as Brooklyn is concerned, nothing ever could match the events of yesterday, when all the years of frustration and defeat were wiped out in one blazing afternoon. It was the 49th Dodger Series game in eight appearances, and the tightest, most tense and thrilling of them all.

At the finish, when Pee Wee Reese sure-handedly threw out Elston Howard, the big park in the Bronx exploded with human emotion as the entire Dodger team raced out on the field and danced and drooled in delight around Podres.

While the 62,465 customers were cheering the new champs, the proud Yankees were filing slowly into the losing dressing room; a unique experience for them. Of all, only coaches Frank Crosetti and Bill Dickey and shortstop Phil Rizzuto had ever experienced a loss before. They had it but once, when the

Cardinals smeared the Yankees four in a row after losing the 1942 opener.

Numerous records were set, but the one the Brooklyn players will remember most was their achievement in winning four of the last five games after dropping the first two. This kind of comeback had never happened in a seven-game Series before.

The drama in this seventh game of the Series heightened in the sixth inning, as the Dodgers scored a run in the top half to take a 2-0 lead. Then, in the Yanks half with Martin and McDougald on, came the

World Series Figures

SEVENTH-GAME FIGURES
Paid attendance—62,465
Net receipts—$407,549.81
Commissioner's share—$61,132.47
Clubs' and leagues' share—$346,417.34

SEVEN-GAME TOTALS
Paid attendance—362,310
Net receipts—$2,337,515.34
Commissioner's share—$350,627.30
Players' share (first four games only)—$654,853.59
Clubs' and leagues' share—$1,332,034.45

GREAT CATCH BY SANDY BROKE YANKEES' BACK
by Dana Mozley

Wednesday, October 5, 1955—Perhaps because of a breeze that grew in the Bronx, a world's championship flag can now be raised in Brooklyn for the first time. Certainly the one play that broke the Yankees' back was Sandy Amoros' great sixth-inning catch and resultant double play. He said an incoming wind held the ball just long enough for him to catch it.

It was a truly fine grab in just the area that has caused so many left fielders so much woe. Most of them running toward the corner where the box seats jut out to the foul line keep one eye on the ball and one eye on the fence. So often the fence wins.

Amoros never bothered about the railing and seats because he never saw them. Starting from left center, where everyone must play Yogi Berra, he raced pell-mell after the ball. That was his only thought.

"I kept my eyes on the ball . . . never looked anywhere else," Sandy explained. "It stayed up just long enough to fall into my glove like this," he added, holding his right hand straight out. "I never hit the fence, but I was only this far from it" . . . and he held his two hands about 20 inches apart.

Reese, who was the middleman on the double play that disrupted a dangerous two-on, none-out situation, said he saw McDougald out of the corner of his eye already at second base. No one had to tell him to throw to first for the twin killing.

Hodges, who completed the DP, had this to say, "What made the play so great, besides Sandy's catch, of course, were the two perfect throws."

key play, the one which probably meant the title. Stengel, disdaining a bunt with Berra up, had Yogi swing away. Podres pitched outside and Berra stroked a long high fly into the left-field corner. Amoros, playing him far over toward center, had to run over 100 feet. The ball stayed up a long time, being held by the wind, and Sandy just reached it, gloving it with his right mitt in fair territory.

Martin and McDougald, not believing a catch possible, were on their horses. Billy suddenly reversed himself when almost to third, and Gil was past second base before he found out the ball had been held. Amoros gracefully whirled and fired to Reese, who went into short left for the throw. Pee Wee then made another perfect throw to Hodges, just getting McDougald as he slid back. That was the 12th Brooklyn DP, a new Series record.

As the Yanks came up in the ninth for their last chance, with right-handed power hitters looming, the Dodger fans stayed seated and the Yankee adherents shouted for a rally. Everyone was excited.

Skowron cracked a sizzler back at Podres, the hard grounder sticking in his glove web. He was unable to get it out for a second or so, and started to run toward first base to make the putout that way. But he was able to pry it loose and make an underhand toss to Hodges. Cerv then hit a high fly which Amoros took in short left, and the Dodgers were one out away from the promised land.

Podres went to 2-2 on Howard and then made him swing off stride at the change-up. Reese took one happy step toward the grounder, aimed it for Hodges, and, though the toss was a bit low, Gil kept his foot on the base and the Dodgers had finally arrived in paradise. ∎

October 5, 1955

Dodgers Delirious— Yanks Take It In Stride

by Jim McCulley

The last shreds of invincibility torn from their proud shoulders, the present-day Yankees—beaten out of a pennant last year, and now for the first time in WS history by the Dodgers—accepted their final undressing yesterday by the Brooks in a most philosophical mood. Nobody kicked in a locker, and nobody quit in disgust over the unprecedented situation.

Yankee president Dan Topping told Stengel:

"Well, Case, it looks like we'll have to learn how the other half lives for a while."

Co-owner Del Webb offered his condolences with: "These things are always tough to take, but we can't win 'em all."

Hank Bauer and Yogi Berra, two of the older members of the team, thought the Yanks went down without a spot of disgrace, and Bauer said: "Maybe it's a good omen. Now we can start all over again." ■

Four of the Yankee sluggers line up with their lumber awaiting "play ball" in the 1955 Series opener. Bill Skowron, Hank Bauer, Yogi Berra, and Eddie Robinson are the would-be bombers. (News photo by Tom Watson.)

Editorial

October 1, 1955—Debate over the wisdom of Jackie Robinson's steal of home in the first game of the Series still rages. But did anyone notice how Yank catcher Yogi Berra effectively blocked Frank Kellert from swinging at Whitey Ford's pitch—a flagrant violation of baseball's rules?

Umpire Bill Summers called Jackie safe, and Yogi called Summers lots of other things, most of them unprintable. The fact is that Jackie WAS safe. The official baseball rules say that "each runner, other than the batter, may without liability of being put out advance one base when, while he is attempting to steal a base, the batter is interfered with by the catcher."

The unique photo sequence of Jackie Robinson's steal of home in Game 1 of the 1955 World Series was captured by *Daily News* photographer Frank Hurley.

DAILY ✚ NEWS

NEW YORK'S PICTURE NEWSPAPER

FINAL

4¢ IN CITY LIMITS

Vol. 38. No. 91   Copr. 1956 News Syndicate Co. Inc.   New York 17, N.Y., Tuesday, October 9, 1956   WEATHER: Fair, windy, cool.

ZERO HERO!

Larsen Drubs Dodgers, 2-0; 1st Perfect Game in 34 Yrs.

Story on page 80

"It's never happened in World Series history, and it hasn't happened since."

5

1956: One Perfect Day

	G	AB	R	H	2B	3B	HR	RBI	BB	SB	BA	SA
1956:	140	521	93	155	29	2	30	105	65	3	.298	.534

The year 1956 will forever be etched in sports history as the year of Don Larsen's perfect game. With an unlikely hero on the mound and a future Hall of Famer behind the plate, Larsen and Berra teamed up for one of the most astonishing athletic feats ever. And it occurred on the World Series stage, with millions of fans hanging on every pitch.

As history records Don Larsen as the owner of this unmatched achievement, it also acknowledges Yogi as the architect of this feat. After the game, Larsen remarked that he at times had been so nervous "Yogi had to do my thinking for me." And when asked about the pitches Yogi called for him during the game, Larsen answered, "I shook Yogi off a couple of times, but that was just to confuse the Dodger batters. I came back with the same pitches I shook off."

Calling the perfect game, however, was not Yogi's only—or even his greatest—contribution to the Yankees' 1956 championship series. Pitted against the Yanks' fiercest rival, the Brooklyn Dodgers, Yogi hit a grand slam in Game 2 and crushed two homers in Game 7 to help clinch the Yankees' 17th World Championship. Yogi's three homers off Dodger star Don Newcombe and his 10 RBIs during the 1956 series were career bests—for a man who still holds many of the career records for World Series play.

Yogi's World Series heroics earned him the title "one of the three best-known Italians in the world — Columbus, Marconi, and Berra" from his St. Louis friends on The Hill. But Yogi's greatest thrill in 1956 came as the year was about to close, when his third son, Dale, was born in December. ∎

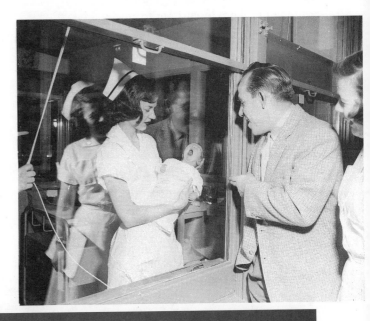

A YOUNG BAWL PLAYER ANNOUNCES HIMSELF. Yankee catcher Yogi Berra gets a look at his howling son, Dale, held by nurse Ruth Woodward in Valley Hospital, Ridgewood, N.J., yesterday.

October 9, 1956

Larsen, Still Wobbling, Gives Credit to Berra

by Dana Mozley

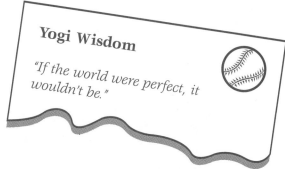

Yogi Wisdom

"If the world were perfect, it wouldn't be."

He looked cool and pitched cool, but Don Larsen was numbed by the jitters in the best game he ever pitched. "I was so nervous I couldn't think straight," the big Swede admitted afterward. "Yogi had to do my thinking for me."

The 6'4", 220-pound right-hander who changed his pitching style only two weeks ago to confuse a sign-stealing coach, was aware from the sixth inning on that he had a perfect game going—the first in 34 years.

"NO ONE HAD to tell me that," he said. "The guys on the bench started snubbing me. The closest I got to any conversation from then on was Yogi's signs.

"I tried to think things out in the last inning, but all I did was think about too many things. I couldn't even tell you what they are now. My arm was still strong, but my legs began to wobble. They're still wobbling now."

HE PUT A FASTBALL past Dale Mitchell to lock up the classic performance. Fastballs and sliders, with an occasional slow curve, were what he served.

"They hit my sliders," he confessed. "Every ball that was hit hard—Amoros' foul home run, Hodges' long drive that Mantle saved, and Snider's line drive the first time up—came off that pitch."

"I liked his fastball best," Berra said; "it was faster than I've seen it. The only two times he shook off my sign, I asked for a fastball. I came right back with the same sign and he struck out Reese [first inning] and Hodges [second inning]."

MR. PERFECT. Yankee pitcher Don Larsen sits outside the Stadium in the new sports car he won for being named the 1956 World Series MVP.

Larsen admitted he was scared when Amoros lined the ball down the right-field line in the fifth. It just curved outside the pole.

"He was out in front of a good slider," the pitcher recalled. "When it started out I was sure I'd lost both the no-hitter and the lead. When it reached right field, I still wasn't sure until the umpire made his decision. What a relief!

"Larsen: Berra Masterminded It"

"That wasn't my only tough moment, however," he added. "Hodges hit one real good and Mickey made a great play. Carey and McDougald also saved me. When you give credit for a game like this, a lot has to go to the fielders and to Yogi."

ALTHOUGH MANTLE'S catch of Hodges' liner in deep left center looked like a great one to everyone else, Mickey shrugged it off. "I was playing him deep to begin with," he explained. "I got a pretty good jump and I was sure I'd get it easier than I did."

Of the baseball brass, the first to congratulate the "perfect" pitcher was Walter O'Malley, the Brook president. "Even though you beat us, I have to give you the very best," he told him.

YANKEE CO-OWNERS Del Webb and Dan Topping were next to elbow their way to the pitcher. "We suffered right with you," Webb told him.

Later, while Larsen was trying to think of the closest he'd been previously to a no-hitter, Jackie Robinson arrived. Shaking hands, Jackie told Don, "I'm still a youngster in this game, but this was by far the finest pitching performance I've ever seen."

"IT'S A LOT TOUGHER to pitch a perfect game," Larsen concluded. "I got so nervous today that I know if anyone ever got on base by a walk or any other way, I might have gone, right then and there." ■

October 9, 1956

History Is Made in Series Classic, Larsen Hurls Perfect Game, Wins, 2-0

by Joe Trimble

The imperfect man pitched a perfect game yesterday. Don Larsen, a free soul who loves the high life, retired all 27 Dodgers in the classic pitching performance of all time as the Yankees won the fifth game, 2-0, at the Stadium and took a 3-2 edge in the set. In this first perfect World Series game, he made but 97 pitches, threw three balls to only one batter, and fanned seven. A man must be lucky as well as good to reach such an incredible height, and Don got four breaks, a "foul homer" which missed being fair by inches and three superb fielding plays on line drives.

This was the first perfect game pitched since right-hander Charley Robertson of the White Sox did it against Detroit on April 30, 1922. Larsen's was the first Series no-hitter, of course. There have been three one-hitters. Don, an affable, nerveless man who laughs his way through life, doesn't know how to worry. And that was his greatest asset in the pressure cauldron that was the big Bronx ball park in the late innings, with the crowd of 64,519 adding to the mounting tension with swelling roars and cheers as one grim-faced Dodger after another failed to break through his serves.

With the tension tearing at their nerves and sweat breaking out on the palms of the onlookers, Larsen seemed to be the calmest man in the place. He knew he had a perfect game and was determined to get it. In the ninth inning, though inwardly tense, he kept perfect control of himself and the ball. Only when pinch hitter Dale Mitchell was called out on strikes to become the 27th dead Dodger did Larsen show emotion.

A GRIN BROKE across his face as Yogi Berra dashed up to him. Berra jumped wildly into Don's arms, the pitcher grabbing and carrying the catcher like a baby for a few strides. Then the entire Yankee bench engulfed the pair of them, and ushers and cops hustled the ball players off the field and into the safety of the dugout before the crowd could get at them.

The Yankee fielders ran up to shake his hand and Don had a special hug for Mickey Mantle, whose fourth-inning homer had given him a lead and whose great catch of a liner by Gil Hodges had saved things in the fifth.

ANDY CAREY, who has been the sloppiest man in the Series afield, also helped on two plays. The third baseman deflected Jack Robinson's liner in the second inning, leaping and pawing the ball to short-stop Gil McDougald, who made the throw to first in time. The play wasn't close.

Carey's other contribution came in the eighth, when the pressure was on everybody. Hodges was the hitter then, too. Gil took a half swing and hit a low liner, which Andy gloved one-hand, bobbled a bit and then held while on the run.

THE OTHER NOD from Lady Luck didn't involve a fielder. In the fifth inning, Sandy Amoros drove a screaming liner into the right-field stands. But it veered to the right side of the foul pole, missing by about four inches. Larsen then got the little Dodger to ground out to Billy Martin and end the inning.

EARLIER in the inning, with one out in the fifth, Hodges had crashed a long line drive to left-center. Mantle raced over and made a spectacular backhand catch on the full run. That ball would have been a homer in Brooklyn, as it was hit over 380 feet.

In the eighth, Larsen made his lone fielding play when he grabbed Robinson's hard hopper with his glove hand. Then it was that Hodges stroked the liner which Carey intercepted a few inches off the ground, juggled while leaning over and running, and then held. The spectators shouted wildly when Don completed the inning with a soft flyout by Amoros.

THE CROWD GAVE Larsen a tremendous hand when he came up to bat in the eighth, standing up to applaud. Then, after the Yankees were retired, he went back to the mound to get the last three outs—the three men who stood between him and baseball immortality.

The Dodgers, still trying to win, dug in. Carl Furillo fouled off a couple and then flied to Hank Bauer in right field. Campy belted a long drive into the upper left-field seats but it was foul by many yards, then grounded weakly to Martin. Mitchell then came up to bat for Maglie, and the Stadium rocked with roars of anticipation.

THE FIRST PITCH to the left-swinger was a fast one which was on the outside, high. Then Don got a low curve over for a strike. Then another fast ball which Mitchell swung at and missed.

Now, for the first time, Larsen was visibly affected. There he stood, one strike away from the most amazing feat in Series history. Don stepped off the mound, turned around to look at the outfielders, and took off his hat. Then he threw another curve that Mitch fouled.

CASEY STENGEL then moved two of the outfielders, Mantle and Bauer, a few feet to the left. Mitchell, a slap hitter, seldom pulls the ball to right. Besides, Berra was going to call for a fastball.

Don, who pitches without windup, then made his next throw, a fastball letter-high, and as Pinelli's right hand went up, the whole baseball world exploded.

The fans at radio and TV sets all over the nation knew it was a perfect game all the way. Announcers Vin Scully and Mel Allen didn't try to disguise it in that silly superstition that to talk about it would jinx the pitcher.

SO, AN INCREDIBLE character who laughs at training rules, reads comic books, and describes himself as "the night rider" has become the classic pitcher in all baseball legend. ■

Baseball's Perfect Games

John Richmond, Worcester vs. Cleveland (NL), 1-0	June 12, 1880
Monte Ward, Providence vs. Buffalo (NL), 5-0	June 17, 1880
Cy Young, Boston vs. Philadelphia (AL), 3-0	May 5, 1904
Addie Joss, Cleveland vs. Chicago (AL), 1-0	October 2, 1908
Ernie Shore, Boston vs. Washington (AL), 4-0	June 23, 1917
Charles Robertson, Chicago vs. Detroit (AL), 2-0	April 30, 1922
x-Don Larsen, Yankees vs. Brooklyn (NL), 2-0	October 8, 1956
Jim Bunning, Philadelphia vs. New York (NL), 6-0	June 21, 1964
Sandy Koufax, Los Angeles vs. Chicago (NL), 1-0	September 9, 1965
Catfish Hunter, Oakland vs. Minnesota (AL), 4-0	May 8, 1968
Len Barker, Cleveland vs. Toronto (AL), 3-0	May 15, 1981
Mike Witt, California vs. Texas (AL), 1-0	September 30, 1984
Tom Browning, Cincinnati vs. Los Angeles (NL), 1-0	September 16, 1988
Dennis Martinez, Montreal vs. Los Angeles (NL), 2-0	July 28, 1991
Kenny Rogers, Texas vs. California (AL), 4-0	July 28, 1994
David Wells, Yankees vs. Minnesota, 4-0	May 17, 1998

x—World Series

YANKEE NO-HITTERS

George Mogridge at Boston, 2-1	April 24, 1917
Sam Jones at Philadelphia, 2-0	September 4, 1923
Monte Pearson vs. Cleveland, 13-0	August 27, 1938
Allie Reynolds at Cleveland, 1-0	July 12, 1951
Allie Reynolds vs. Boston, 8-0	September 28, 1951
x-Don Larsen vs. Brooklyn, 2-0	October 8, 1956
Dave Righetti vs. Boston, 4-0	July 4, 1983
y-Andy Hawkins vs. Chicago, 0-4	July 1, 1990
Jim Abbott vs. Cleveland, 4-0	September 4, 1993
Dwight Gooden vs. Seattle, 2-0	May 14, 1996
z-David Wells vs. Minnesota, 4-0	May 17, 1998

x-perfect game in World Series
y-Hawkins lost when Chicago scored four runs on three Yankee errors
z-perfect game

Our Man Been Here, Seen This

by Bill Madden

May 18, 1998—I was 11 years old that Oct. 8 afternoon in 1956 when my father hugged me—and just about everyone else around us in the left-field upper deck of Yankee Stadium—and nearly began crying. On the field, Yogi Berra was jumping into Don Larsen's arms and delirium reigned.

"A perfect game!" my father screamed. "A perfect game! We're all going to be famous!"

Later, as we walked across the McCombs Dam bridge to our car, my father said: "You had quite a thrill for your first World Series game, didn't you? I guarantee you'll never see anything like that again!"

Who was I to doubt him? I mean, really, what are the chances of anyone seeing two perfect games, in the same ball park, in his or her lifetime? To the best of my knowledge there were only three other people besides myself at Yankee Stadium for David Wells' perfect game yesterday who were also there for Larsen's 42 years ago—Bob Sheppard, the Yankees' public-address announcer; Don Zimmer; and Joe Torre. Zimmer, the Yankees' bench coach, was on the Dodger bench that day in 1956 and Torre, like me, was in the upper deck in left field.

When I told Larsen that yesterday, he laughed. "Yeah," he said, "you and about 10 million other people who claimed they were there."

But I have the scorecard, autographed years later by Larsen, to prove it. It's hard to forget your first World Series game, especially when it turns out to be one for the ages.

Like Torre, the play I most remember about Larsen's perfect game was Mickey Mantle's catch off Gil Hodges in left-center. It was about the only hard-hit ball the Dodgers had in the entire game. The only other "scare" for Larsen was Jackie Robinson's hard shot to third that glanced off Andy Carey's glove to Gil McDougald, who made the throw over to first for the out.

Larsen needed only 97 pitches for his perfect game to Wells' 120 yesterday. But Wells was more dominating. Afterward, Twins manager Tom Kelly was at a loss to single out anything that had even a chance of being a base hit.

After witnessing Wells' feat, I'd like to tell you I've seen everything now. But that's what my father told me, too, and what did he know?)

PICTURE STILL IS PERFECTLY CLEAR TO YOGI

by Mike Lupica

May 19, 1998—Once Yogi Berra was one of the most famous baseball pictures of all. This was before every highlight was a piece of television tape, before we preserved our sports memories that way. This picture, from October 1956, was black and white, a still, the way Willie Mays with his back to home plate, cap off his head, was a black-and-white still in October 1954. This was Yogi jumping into Don Larsen's arms. Larsen threw the perfect game. Yogi became the perfect picture.

Now it was 42 years later at Yankee Stadium, and Jorge Posada was running for Wells and Yogi didn't know anything about it. He had been in Pittsburgh on this afternoon with his son Dale. There was a 5:30 flight home. Yogi stood in the gate area and signed one autograph after another, right until he got on the plane.

He walked into his house about 8 o'clock and the first thing his wife, Carmen, said was, "Did you hear?"

"Hear what?"

"David Wells pitched a perfect game for the Yankees. How could you not hear?"

"Carmen," he said, "there wasn't a radio on the plane."

He sat down in front of the television and eventually was able to watch some of the highlights from Wells' amazing day at Yankee Stadium. Only then it became another day at the Stadium for Yogi, from 1956. The last strike on Dale Mitchell. That run for the pitcher's mound. That leap into Larsen's arms that is as much a history of the day as anything.

Larsen's perfect game. Yogi's perfect picture.

"The best it ever got," Yogi said yesterday. "How could you ever beat perfect?"

"As soon as my wife told me, I went right back to that day," he said. "How could you not?"

He was asked what he remembers best about the day.

"Everything," Yogi Berra said.

He was asked if he got nervous as the game wore on, the way ball players have gotten nervous for all games like this across baseball history, afraid that one mistake could ruin everything.

"It was a 2-0 ball game, remember," Yogi said. "Sal Maglie was pitching pretty good himself. Larsen only ended up throwing 97 pitches. There was never any time to be nervous."

He said he did worry about a walk, about Larsen going to ball three late in the game. He remembered the game in the '47 Series when Floyd Bevens had a no-hitter and then walked the whole ball park, 10 for the game, the last two right before Cookie Lavagetto broke up the no-hitter and beat the Yankees with a double. And he remembered the two no-hitters he had caught from Allie Reynolds before he was behind the plate for Larsen.

"A no-hitter is always special," he said. "A perfect game is something that only comes along once in your life."

Twice in the life of Yankee Stadium. First with Larsen, out of Point Loma High School in San Diego. Now with Wells, also out of Point Loma High School. Perfect games are not always pitched by baseball's greatest stars. Sometimes, though, these days seem to have been made in the stars.

Yogi was told about David Cone walking down to Wells in the dugout and breaking everybody up by saying, "I think it's time to break out the knuckleball."

"Did he do that?" Yogi said. "Man, nobody went near Larsen, not one time the whole game. We let him sit down there by himself." He laughed and said, "Oh, man, that Cone."

Yogi Berra and Don Larsen are still friends. They will see each other soon at an appearance for a pharmaceutical company in Kansas City. Whitey Ford will be there, some other old Yankees. And the pitcher-catcher combination from Oct. 8, 1956. From that picture that has them together forever at the mound at the Stadium.

After Wells' game on Sunday, he was connected to Larsen by the telephone, put in his hand in Joe Torre's office. The connection between Larsen and Berra is forever.

Yogi was asked yesterday if there has ever been a time in the four decades since the game when he and Larsen have gotten together and not talked about it.

"Are you kidding?" he said. "We talk about it with each other and then people want to talk about it with us, especially once we go to the bar. It was one of those things, you know? One of those things that happen in baseball people talk about the rest of your life."

There were more pictures at Yankee Stadium Sunday, without the shadows the place gets in October. There was more history. Just not like the history Don Larsen and Yogi Berra had once. Just not like their picture.

4 Yankee Homers Bludgeon Dodgers, 9-0

Berra Hits Pair, Skowron Slams; Kucks 3-Hits, Newk Walloped

by Dick Young

The Brooks' benign reign as champions of all the baseball world ended yesterday, just one year after it began—and the title returns to the Yankees, who claim it by divine right. The Brooks didn't abdicate—they were assassinated. They were tied up and gagged by a culprit named Johnny Kucks, who held them to three singles. They were bludgeoned to bits by homer-hitter Yogi Berra, who blasted two, by Elston Howard, who took a solo swing, and by Bill Skowron, who made it a bloody 9-0 mess by walloping a grand-slammer.

Today, the Brooks, or what's left of them, flee to the Orient . . . and how are they going to explain this one in Japanese? It doesn't even make sense in Brooklynese. Can they explain how, after blasting their way to victory in the first two games, they lost four of the next five? Can they explain that, in the last three games, they scored a grand total of one run, and accumulated seven hits? Can they explain that they, the power guys, batted .195 for the Series?

The Yankees' victory was their 17th World Series triumph out of 22.

It was one of the most amazing turnabouts in memory. The Yankees, with a pitching staff that hadn't turned in four consecutive complete games at any time during the season, and with a staff that had used up 11 hurlers in the first two scraps of the Series, suddenly came up with five straight completions by five different hurlers.

AMONG THESE was Don Larsen's historic perfect performance in game No. 5, and Kucks' three-hitter yesterday.

CASEY STENGEL, ironically, had considered Kucks a distinct risk. Johnny, although an 18-victory

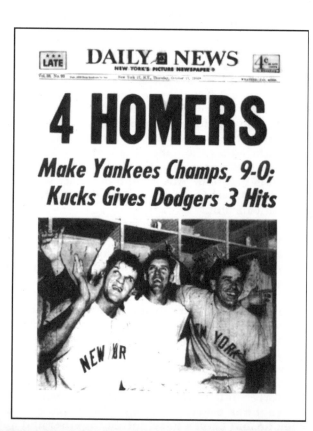

THE WIN'S BEHIND THEM. Bill Skowron, Johnny Kucks, and Yogi Berra (l. to r.) smile it up in the Yankees' dressing room after their amalgamated efforts won the seventh game of the World Series, 9-0, at Ebbets Field. Skowron hit a bases-loaded homer, Kucks limited the Dodgers to three hits, and Berra drove home the first four runs with a pair of homers.

man during the season, hadn't won a game since Labor Day. Before Kucks made a pitch yesterday, Casey had Tom Sturdivant warming up in the pen. And at the end, with the score 9-0, Casey had Ford and Grim firing.

ON THE OTHER HAND, there was Don Newcombe . . . but not for long. Only slightly longer than he had lasted in the second game, when the Yanks blasted him out with six runs by the second inning. Then, it was a homer by Berra that finished off Newk. This time, Don hung around long enough for Yogi to hit two.

Bauer had opened the game with a hit to left-center and had stolen second. Newk steadied, whiffed Martin and Mantle, and pushed across two strikes on Yogi . . . both fouled . . . off change-ups. Then, Newk tried to get a fast ball past Berra.

YOGI HATCHETED at the high buzzer, and the ball soared across the street and into one of those parking lots which are the source of so much trouble to Newcombe.

WINNING DOUBLE. Kucks and Berra come together in the Yank dressing room after the game. They teamed up in the game, too, and that's what killed Brooklyn.

Don then whiffed Skowron on three pitches, and the inning ended with Newk having struck out the side . . . but trailing, 2-0. He was throwing numerous strikes. He was ahead of everyone, in fact, except the Yanks.

Berra next came up in the third. Again, there were two out. Again there was a man on. Billy Martin had singled up the middle, past Reese's dive.

AGAIN NEWK got ahead of Berra, 1-and-2. Again he tried a fastball—this time low. Yogi, who doesn't know high from low, and cares less, golfed it over the scoreboard in right-center.

This gave Yogi 10 RBIs, for the Series—which is a record surpassing the nine banged by Lou Gehrig in '28. It also gave Yogi three homers for this set, and nine in his World Series life. ■

Series Figures

SEVENTH GAME FIGURES
Attendance—33,782
Net receipts—$223,828.80
Commissioner's share—$33,574.32
Clubs' and leagues' share—$190,254.48

SEVEN-GAME TOTALS
Attendance—345,903
Net receipts—$2,183,254.59
Commissioner's share—$326,988.20
Clubs' and leagues' share—$1,180,204.70
(Players shared in only the first four games—$693,561.53)

October 11, 1956

Don Didn't Choke

by Dana Mozley

"Now they'll be saying, more than ever, that he chokes up," Jackie Robinson fumed. "No one in the world should say it, but they will. That son of a gun was throwing as hard today as I've ever seen him. Choking up . . . my back!"

This was one man's sentiment about Don Newcombe's failures once again to win the big game. Roy Campanella agreed. So did Pee Wee Reese, Duke Snider, Gil Hodges, and all the other beaten Brooks.

"Sure, his control wasn't perfect," Campy went on, "but he didn't make all the mistakes he seemed to make. Berra hit that first home run off his chin. It was two strikes and Newk was just wasting one. I guess you have to hit Yogi to keep him from hitting you. You can't throw it bad enough by him."

The second home run was a mistake—by Newcombe. He put another fastball on the inside corner of the plate, while again trying to brush Yogi back in a ball-one, strike-two situation.

"Man, that Berra is a killer," Campy complained. "All Newcombe has to do is get a third strike past him and he's probably pitching yet. Mantle? You saw how big Newk threw those strikes past him. Struck him out twice, didn't he?"

Many wondered what Reese had said to Newcombe when he went to the mound in the first inning, just before Yogi homered off the 0-2 pitch.

"I warned him," Pee Wee said, "that if he threw a change-up [the Brooks like to throw slow ones to Yogi] to make sure it was outside the plate. Instead, he throws a fastball, high and inside, and Yogi parks it." ▪

Downcast, Newcombe leaves the game muttering something about Berra. Yogi hit three homers against Newk in the 1956 World Series.

Yogi's Father Expected It

St. Louis, October 11, 1956—Pietro Berra, a man of pride, sat in silence today when his son Yogi hit a pair of two-run homers to send the Yankees off to a fast start toward their victory in the deciding World Series game.

"He was thrilled but he didn't say anything much," said Yogi's sister, Mrs. Josephine Sadowski.

"He expected his son to do that," said Mrs. Sadowski of the batting that gave Yogi a record-breaking 10 runs batted in for the Series.

The elder Berra, who speaks English with a heavy Italian accent, begrudged every out while the Yankees were at bat—despite their lopsided 9-0 triumph over Brooklyn.

Pete Berra and other members of the family watched the TV broadcast of the game at their home in the Italian section of St. Louis known as The Hill.

WIRES TO BOTH

October 11, 1956—Mayor Wagner had words of praise for both the champ Yanks and the beaten Brooks after yesterday's Series finale.

In one wire, addressed to co-owners Dan Topping and Del Webb, manager Casey Stengel, and the Yankee team, he said: "Heartiest congratulations to the 1956 World Series champions on your wonderful victory today. All New Yorkers are proud and happy for you. My greetings and best wishes to every member of the team."

In the other telegram, to Dodger owner Walter O'Malley, manager Walt Alston, captain Pee Wee Reese, and the Dodger team, the Mayor said: "It was a great fight while it lasted and there's always next year. My congratulations to all the Dodgers for their great spirit and skill. New Yorkers are proud of you."

Berra Honored by 'Hill' Friends

The champion Yankees' star catcher was honored by his friends on "The Hill" here today as "one of the three best-known Italians in the world—Columbus, Marconi, and Yogi Berra."

Berra was feted by the Professional and Businessmen's Club of The Hill, the Italian section from which he emerged as one of baseball's greatest backstops.

Fred Giacoma, vice president of the club, presented Berra with a scroll and made him an honorary member. The Italians and baseball notables praised his contributions to the game and his heroics in the 1956 World Series.

Berra dedicated the two 2-run homers he smashed in the final game at Brooklyn to his mother, who is convalescing from a serious operation. ■

THE CHOKE'S ON HIM. Campanella playfully tightens Yogi Berra's tie after hostilities were recessed till today. Ralph Branca enjoys the fun.

While preparing for the upcoming World Series battle with Brooklyn, Yogi relaxes in a park near his home in Wood Cliff Lake, N.J.

December 21, 1956—THEY'RE IN THE MONEY. Whitey Ford and Yogi Berra hold their new contracts as they leave Yankee Stadium yesterday after signing pacts for the 1957 season. For Yogi, his new contract for $58,000 makes him the top-priced catcher in the American League. Ford signed for $35,000.

"It was hard to have a conversation with anyone, there were so many people talking."

6
1957: At the Copa

	G	AB	R	H	2B	3B	HR	RBI	BB	SB	BA	SA
1957:	134	482	74	121	14	2	24	82	57	1	.251	.438

The Yankees made their biggest headlines in 1957 with their activities off the field. In May, Hank Bauer, Yogi Berra, Whitey Ford, Johnny Kucks, Mickey Mantle, and Billy Martin were involved in an altercation at the Copacabana nightclub. The six players, who were celebrating Martin's birthday at the club, were each fined $1,000 by Yankees president Dan Topping for their part in the brawl. The incident prompted an investigation by the local district attorney, but fortunately for the six, the DA decided not to pursue criminal charges.

Yogi struggled at the plate in 1957, hitting only .251 for the year—a drop of 47 points from the previous season. He briefly tried wearing glasses, but abandoned them because his wife, Carmen, didn't think he needed them. In his fielding, however, he needed no assistance: on July 28, he began a record-setting 148-game errorless streak behind the plate. And, for the fourth consecutive year, he led American League catchers in putouts, with 704.

After the exhilaration of winning the 1956 World Series, the Yankees were brought down to earth by the Milwaukee Braves in 1957. The Braves won the Series in seven games behind the flawless pitching of Lew Burdette. Ironically, Burdette—who won Games 2, 5, and 7—had developed his skills in the Yankee farm system. Yogi batted .320 in the Series, with eight hits and one home run, but the Yankees were unable to overcome injuries to Mantle and Moose Skowron, and the World Championship left New York City for the first time since 1949. ■

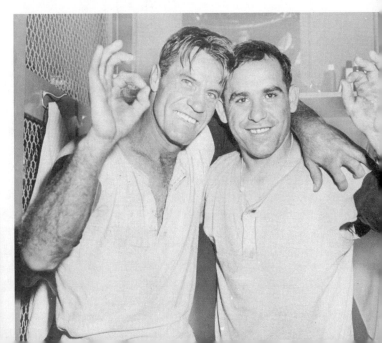

They're smiling now, but Yankee stars Hank Bauer and Yogi Berra had some nervous moments while the local authorities looked into the infamous Copacabana incident. (News photo by Charles Hoff.)

May 17, 1957

Berra and Ford Benched After A.M. Brawl in Copa

by Arthur North and David Quirk

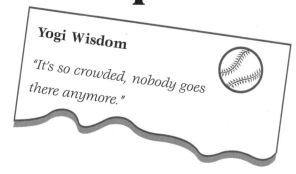

Yogi Wisdom

"It's so crowded, nobody goes there anymore."

An early-morning brawl in the Copacabana cost Whitey Ford his pitching assignment last night and benched catcher Yogi Berra for good measure.

In the nightclub rhubarb, a 40-year-old delicatessen man—and a Yankee rooter to boot—got slugged in the jaw, giving him visions of a $250,000 damage suit against the Copa and the Yanks' burly Hank Bauer, whom he blamed for the blow.

Even angrier than the battle's only casualty, Edwin Jones of 602 W. 18th St., was Yankee manager Casey Stengel.

Just before the game between the Yanks and the Kansas City Athletics, Stengel announced he was taking Whitey off the mound and substituting Bob Turley.

"I won't pitch Ford because the whole world knows he was out until two in the morning," snapped Casey. "He knew days in advance that he was supposed to pitch this game. He had no right to be out after hours. If I pitched him and he was hit hard, people would wonder what I was doing.

"Berra has been around long enough to know better. The way he's been hitting, he could use a rest

IT'S A NO-HITTER FOR HANK. Mickey Mantle, Billy Martin, Hank Bauer, and Hank's wife, Charlene (l. to r.), are happy folks leaving the DA's office after the grand jury refused to indict Hank on charges growing out of the Copa brawl. Delicatessen owner Edwin Jones had claimed Bauer slugged him in the nose. (News photo by Bob Costello.)

Leaving the district attorney's office are (l. to r.) Mickey Mantle, Whitey Ford, Yogi Berra, Mrs. Hank Bauer, Hank himself, and John Kucks. In the background is their attorney, Sidney Friedman. (News photo by Bob Costello.)

instead of being out late. Anyway, with a left-hander pitching against us, I think he can stand a night off."

Casey dropped Bauer to eighth place in the batting order. Mickey Mantle, another of the nightclubbers, also stayed in the lineup.

"I'm not mad enough to take a chance on losing a ball game and possibly the pennant," Stengel explained.

Two other teammates in the party—infielder Billy Martin and pitcher Johnny Kucks—were not scheduled to play last night anyhow.

The fight at the Copa early yesterday climaxed a night on the town by the ball players in honor of Billy Martin's birthday.

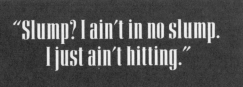

"Slump? I ain't in no slump. I just ain't hitting."

Last night, after Stengel's punitive action and threats by Jones to file suit, the Yankee management issued this statement:

"The Yankees have made a preliminary examination of the facts surrounding Billy Martin's birthday party, which was attended by certain players—all with their wives with the exception of Martin, who is a bachelor—and are convinced that neither Bauer nor any Yankee player struck anyone last night.

"Bauer has engaged counsel of his own and the legal aspects of this matter are in the hands of said counsel."

Bauer's attorney is Sidney O. Friedman of 30 Broad St.

Confined to his bed for at least four days with a broken nose, busted jaw, arm and body bruises, Jones told reporters:

"I love Bauer, Martin, and all of the Yankees. I've been a Yankee fan for years and this incident has disappointed me."

When he then added that he didn't want to "make a case out of it," his lawyer, Anthony E. Zingales, interrupted with: "Don't let your love run away with you."

Jones, whose bowling club was celebrating at the Copa, disclosed that he would proceed with a civil suit and, if X rays showed more serious injuries, with criminal action against the Yankee slugger, known to his teammates as the Bruiser.

Deputy Chief Inspector Edward Feeley, in charge of the investigation of the brawl, said last night that it appeared to be in the misdemeanor class. More witnesses are to be interrogated on what happened, he said. ■

June 4, 1957

Sinning 6 Yanked 1G Each for Copa Caper

by Joe Trimble

The Yankees' Sinning Six discovered over the weekend that they had combined to pick up the most expensive tab in baseball history as a result of their post-midnight spree at the Copacabana the night of May 15, and in private they were hollering plenty.

The six players—Hank Bauer, Mickey Mantle, Yogi Berra, Whitey Ford, Johnny Kucks, and Billy Martin—each were fined $1,000 by Dan Topping, president of the club.

The $6,000 belt was deducted from the paychecks they received last Friday, the 31st of the month. Ball players are paid on the 15th and last day of each month.

They Don't Like It

The highest previous fines for a single incident were $5,000 levies against Babe Ruth for breaking training in 1925 and against Ted Williams for spitting at the fans in Boston last Aug. 7.

The players were bitter at the stiffness of the punishment, and manager Casey Stengel also indicated that the affair might have been handled in a different way.

But Stengel knew of the fines in advance and there is no substance to reports that he is feuding with Topping and George Weiss, the general manager.

"They should be fined, but the ones who make the big money should pay more," Casey said. "You know who I mean. Not a kid like Kucks, who isn't in those high pay brackets."

Called on Carpet

Topping called the six players into Stengel's office adjoining the Yankee dressing room at the Stadium on May 23 and told them they'd have to pay for their indiscretion—but he didn't mention the amount of the fines that would be forthcoming.

Yogi Berra doesn't appear to be the most unhappy guy in Grand Central Station as the Yanks left last night for a 13-game Western trip after being relieved of $1,000, along with five mates for extracurricular activities. (News photo by Hy Rothman.)

So until they saw the deductions from their checks on Friday, none guessed that it would be so severe.

What irks Stengel is that the fines were levied so quickly. Bauer still faces arraignment on an assault charge that night, and the manager is afraid that the outfielder's case may become prejudiced by the breaking of the news.

One of the players who was fined griped openly. "It's a big bite," he said. "You can't expect a guy to be happy about it. Since when is anybody happy about parting with a thousand bucks?"

THE SALARIES of the players involved are Berra, $60,500; Mantle, $60,000; Ford, $35,000; Bauer, $30,000; Martin, $24,000; and Kucks, $13,500.

Martin, Ford, and Mantle all have been fined before, but until Bauer's arraignment, no Yankee had been unlucky enough to have his name grace the police blotter. Past indiscretions have been kept "in the family." ■

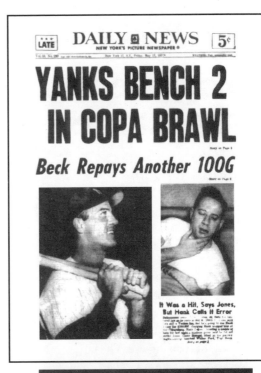

The front page of the *Daily News*, May 17, 1957.

Although the Copacabana incident grabbed most of the headlines early in the 1957 season, Yogi and his Yankee teammates fought hard to keep their focus on the field. Down by six games at the time of the incident, the Yankees went on a seven-game winning streak shortly thereafter to take over first place from the Chicago White Sox. The Yankees marched on to their 23rd pennant—by eight games over the White Sox—and moved on to a World Series showdown with the Milwaukee Braves.

Yogi Learns Specs Prolong His Career

by Joe Trimble

Until a few years ago, some major leaguers who needed glasses were too shortsighted to try them. To don specs indicated a man was slipping—that he was losing his batting eye. The current theory is the reverse—wear 'em to save a career.

This year three of the most prominent players in the AL took their sorry batting averages to their oculists for remedying. Sam White of the Red Sox, the Yanks' Yogi Berra, and Bobby Avila of the Indians all began to wear glasses after consulting opticians.

"I GUESS I RAISED my average 80 points after getting them," Avila said recently. "I had an operation on the white part of my right eye two years ago and the eye grew weaker in that time. I use them for reading and watching television."

Avila was hitting around .190 when he decided on the glasses after refusing to wear them in the first half of the season, and his average climbed to .277 in a month's time.

BERRA'S TROUBLE was diagnosed as "tired eyes." He was told to wear the specs while reading and watching TV in order to rest his optics for baseball. But when his average stayed down around .230, he started to use the glasses in batting practice and then in games. Now he's a confirmed believer.

The Yankee catcher at first thought there was no difference. "I can see as well without 'em at bat," he claimed when other players in his club suggested he wear the specs in games. But he gave 'em a try and found there was a difference. It was graphically proved in a game on July 30, when he made four hits while aided by the glasses and failed to hit the other time up, when he went without them. That game was against Kansas City at Yankee Stadium.

WHITE HAD LOST his job to Pete Daley in the first month of the season, when he made only three hits. So he went to have his eyes examined and his hitting improved to the point where he became the No. 1 receiver of the Bosox again.

Berra's glasses are tinted yellow. Avila has two pair, white and yellow, but prefers the white or natural lenses. Earl Torgeson of the White Sox switches, wearing tinted ones in the bright sun and plain lenses at night.

IN ALL, there are about a dozen regular players, not counting pitchers, who wear specs now; included are such power hitters as Bob Nieman, Baltimore; George Crowe, Cincy; and the Cards' Del Ennis.

Berra wears his only at bat, as does KC catcher Hal Smith. But Tim Thompson, the A's other receiver, and Washington's Clint Courtney wear 'em in the field as well. The mask doesn't hinder them. ■

January 8, 1958—Yogi discarded his glasses. Carmen, his wife, doesn't think he needs them and he agrees. He wore them at bat for about a week last year but they didn't help. "All I need is a few hits and that'll take care of my troubles."

Skowron is the first to greet Berra after Yogi knocked in three of eight runs with his 250th career homer and the 12th of this season. He also collected his 1,000th hit in the game. (News photo by Charles Hoff.)

OUR GUY SAL. Sal Maglie shows his pitching grip to Yanks' catcher Yogi Berra (l.) and Don Larsen in the clubhouse after being acquired from the Dodgers yesterday for pitching insurance during the stretch run. The Barber, what with the Giants moving out, will have the distinction of being the last man to play with all three New York clubs. (News photo by Fred Morgan.)

October 11, 1957

Burdette's 3d Makes Braves Champs

Yankee Error Opens Door to 5-0 Win

by Joe Trimble

Milwaukee brewed the miracle yesterday—winning the world championship with a crashing 5-0 victory over the Yankees at the Stadium. Standing heroically on the mound, Selva Lewis Burdette Jr. lifted the Braves to victory in the seventh game—his second successive blanking of the Bombers and his third triumph in the series.

The 31-year-old right-hander's magnificent seven-hitter brought the title to Milwaukee just five years after the franchise shift from Boston. It served as the trigger for the wildest civic demonstration a baseball-batty burg ever has had. Burdette, the outstanding player in the classic, could be elected chief braumeister of the city—which is better than being Mayor.

The Braves deserved to win. The Yankees deserved to lose. The 61,207 fans showered Burdette with cheers at the finish. Earlier, they had jeered the Yankees, who presented the unusual and pathetic picture of a team beating itself. For the first time in their proud history, the pinstripe perfectionists lost a World Series with their fielding.

They blundered into three errors yesterday, the most damaging one by Tony Kubek, who had been one of the more brilliant Bombers in the early games. That ruined an easy double play which would have gotten Don Larsen out of the third inning. He got out in an unhappier way, as the Braves blasted through the opening for four runs.

Strangely, poor New York glovework figured in all three of Burdette's victories. The Yanks gave the Braves two runs in Lew's 4-2 win here in the second game and Jerry Coleman's boo-boo set up the only score as he won the fifth game, 1-0, in Milwaukee.

It's a good thing they weren't handling the money which piled up in this richest Series in history, which was seen by more people paying more money than ever before. The totals for the seven games were 394,712 spectators and $2,475,978.94 at the gate, after taxes. Highest previous figures were the 389,763 fans who saw the Yanks and Dodgers in 1947 and the "take" of $2,337,515.34 in the '55 set between the same two clubs.

Art Ditmar was pitching for the Yankees in the fourth when Hazle singled after two out and McDougald made a bad throw to second after fielding Logan's grounder. Ditmar got out of the stick mess with luck, Eddie Mathews lashing a liner right at Mantle. Berra made the third Bomber bobble in the fifth, flubbing Aaron's bunt a few feet in front of the plate. The next three men grounded out, the fans mock-cheering the Yankees as they executed ordinary fielding plays.

The Yankees had a fair shot at Burdette in the sixth, after Mantle singled with two out. Berra came up and the crowd stirred in expectation of a homer which would put the Yanks in contention. Instead, Yogi tapped a nubber to third, which Mathews fumbled as he grabbed at it with his mitt hand while stumbling around nervously. This gave McDougald a chance, but Gil topped one of Burdette's "SS" pitches (sinker or spitter?) and forced Mantle at third.

Tommy Byrne was on the mound in the eighth when Crandall hit one into the left-field seats after two were out. Slaughter started slowly, then went full tilt and crashed into the fence as the ball flicked off his mitt.

Burdette went through Bauer, Slaughter, and Mantle without trouble in the eighth, and the crowd began to sense that the reign of the Yankees was about over.

Berra popped to Torre to start the ninth and the fans cheered. McDougald lined a single to center before Kubek's fly to center brought more applause.

Then came the Coleman and Byrne hits, Mathews' final stop and stomp, and the miracle had been wrought. And by a pitcher the Yankees had given up six years ago in a trade with the then Boston Braves. Burdette held his former teammates to two runs in 27 innings and none over the final 24, in the most dominant pitching performance in a Series since Christy Mathewson's three shutouts in 1905—a half century ago. ■

Contest Winner Saturday

As soon as Ed Mathews' speared Bill Skowron's liner to end the World Series at the Stadium yesterday, The News *staff went to work to determine the winner of the $5,000 World Series Contest.*

Still in the running for the $2,500 first prize and the 13 additional cash awards were all fans who picked Milwaukee to win in seven games. The complete list of winners will be printed in The News *tomorrow.*

"You give 100 percent in the first half of the game, and if that isn't enough, in the second half you give what's left."

7
1958: Comeback

	G	AB	R	H	2B	3B	HR	RBI	BB	SB	BA	SA
1958:	122	433	60	115	17	3	22	90	35	3	.266	.471

In 1958, the Yankees avenged their 1957 World Series loss to Milwaukee by coming back from a three-games-to-one deficit to beat the Braves in seven and bring the World Championship back to New York. In the final game, they scored six runs against pitcher Lew Burdette, their nemesis the previous year, to win 6-2 and regain the crown.

In 1958, Yogi set six World Series records, extended four he already held, and tied three others. Among the records Yogi broke were most total Series hits (61); most total Series bases (101); and most putouts by a catcher in one series (60). The two teams broke a total of 18 Series records and tied 15 more.

Yogi also began a new business venture in 1958: he and former teammate Phil Rizzuto opened a 40-lane bowling alley near Yogi's New Jersey home. The bowling alley was just one of many enterprises Yogi would participate in over the years, and proved to be one of the most successful. Over time, Yogi became as famous for his shrewd business moves as he was for his uninhibited playing style. ■

Phil Rizzuto, right, watches as Yogi Berra digs the first shovel of dirt to break ground for their new 40-alley bowling center in Clifton, N.J. (News photo by Leonard Detrick.)

Yanks Champs, Crush Braves 6-2

Turley Hurls 2-Hit Relief; Skowron's HR Clincher

by Dick Young

Milwaukee—They said it couldn't be done. They said that a team down 3-and-1 in the World Series, facing sudden extinction with one more defeat, couldn't win the next three. But the Yankees did it. They wound it up today, 6-2, with a tremendous long-distance relief job by Bob Turley; late-game clutch hits by Yogi Berra and Elly Howard; a crushing eighth-frame homer by Bill Skowron off Lew Burdette; and some earlier fuddle-fingering by the Braves.

So Milwaukee now returns the baseball crown to New York, whence it came last October. This is the 18th time the Yankees have become champions of all the baseball universe and outer space, and none has come harder. Only once before—33 years ago, in fact—had a team made such a stimulating comeback: the Pirates against the Senators with the same sort of three-game rebound.

There was a general feeling that the Yankee dynasty had had it. Along about last Sunday, when the Yanks were down 3-and-1, and everyone was wondering whether the Series would return to Milwaukee, you heard mutterings about the rebuilding job that fated George Weiss, and Lee MacPhail, and Stengel and the rest. Do these Yanks look washed up?

Bob Turley, who blanked the Braves on Monday to make the Series 3-and-2; who relieved the next game and got the final out to make the Series 3-and-3; who relieved Don Larsen again today, as early

as the third inning, and gave just two hits, one a homer by Crandall, as he powered the rest of the way.

And Yogi Berra, who has lots of baseball left in him at age 33. He blasted the double, a near homer,

McDougald, Berra, and Bauer (l. to r.) were pictures of determination before yesterday's Game 7 against the Milwaukee Braves. Their stern looks gave way to smiles of joy as the Yankees completed their improbable comeback with a 6-2 win over the Braves. (News photo by Fred Morgan.)

that ignited the four-run, title-winning eighth against Burdette.

And Elly Howard, who has even more baseball left in him. He banged the hit that sent Berra home with the tie snapper.

And Bill Skowron, who is big and strong, and only 28. He blasted the homer that scored three more in the eighth, and resigned the highly Brave-flavored crowd of 46,367 that one year of miracles was all Lew Burdette was entitled to.

The Braves had scored a run on a small hit in the first, so the Yanks came right back and topped them with two runs on no hits. It was here, in the second, that Torre had his worst time since he flunked the math quiz at James Madison HS in Brooklyn.

Berra had walked to open the inning. Howard pushed a bunt down the right side. Torre fielded the ball, and Burdette rushed over to cover first. Torre, instead of leading Lew with the toss, undershot him. Burdette reached back awkwardly with his glove. The ball dribbled down his leg, tangled in his feet as Lew crossed the bag, and rolled free. It wasn't far enough for Howard to go to second, but sufficient for Berra to take third.

The Braves seemed to like that play so much, they tried it again when Lumpe followed with a topper to the right side. Torre scooped up the ball, poised his arm as though to fire home, then noticed that Yogi wasn't trying to score.

Burdette, meanwhile, was on the move to cover first. Torre turned and flipped behind Lew. It was almost an impossible angle. Burdette contorted his body, reaching back in one direction while his legs were carrying him in another—across the bag. Again, the ball dribbled to the ground, the bases were loaded, and Torre, normally a fine fielder, was looking for a hole in which to climb.

One run came across as Skowron banged into a force at second and outlegged the DP try. The other came in on Kubek's substantial line-out to Covington in left. Howard tagged up and crossed unchallenged on that one.

And it was 2-1 Yankees, with runs that were gift-wrapped in a bright ribbon.

When Crandall came up in the sixth with the score still 2-1 Yanks, there were two down; none on. He was determined. He came up swinging. He went for Turley's first serve and pumped it over the left-field fence. He had homered in the last game of the last

Series, too. That time it had been just an embellishing run. This was a big one; it tied the score, 2-2.

Now the natives were excited. They whooped it up for each Yankee out, anticipating the time that one of the Braves would break it open. Burdette, after all, was pitching splendidly. He had given just two hits till then—McDougald's double to left-center in the third; Howard's loop single to right to open the fourth.

When Burdette looks back on the 1958 Series, he will see the eighth inning, when he got the first two men so easily and anticipation was in his every pitch.

And then he'll see:

That double by Berra, which came within three feet of clearing the right corner of the grandstand for a homer; that four-bouncer up the middle by Howard, a hit that had eyes and delivered the tie-breaking run; that crack off Ed Mathews' glove by Andy Carey, who had become a sixth-inning sub at third for Lumpe and who was more than a defensive replacement.

And finally, Lew will see Skowron's homer flying over the left-center fence and high into the bleachers. Four straight hits; four straight runs.

Lew was allowed to finish the inning; then Don McMahon came in with a mop and soaked up the blood of the Braves and the tears of their fans. ∎

Berra Sets 6 Marks, Extends 4, and Ties 3

Yogi Berra of the Yankees set six records, extended four he already held, and tied three others in the 1958 World Series. In all, 18 marks were shattered and 15 tied by the Yanks and Braves.

Among the records Berra eclipsed were most hits, total Series (61); most total bases, total Series (101); and most putouts by a catcher in one series (60).

Yanks Sign Berra At a $2,500 Cut

by Joe Trimble

Yogi Berra took a "cut" yesterday and got only a piece of the ball. That is, the Yankee catcher signed his contract at a reduction, the first in his 12 years with the Bombers. He'll get about $58,000, a drop of $2,500 from last year, which was his worst in the majors.

He hadn't expected it but he wasn't resentful after Lee MacPhail explained the club's attitude. "Our payroll is the highest in the majors," said the assistant GM and director of playing personnel. "We have to give some deserved raises to men who had good years and so we have to try to balance things by cutting those who didn't. We try to keep the thing in line as much as possible."

BERRA ADMITTED he wasn't so hot last year. "Sure, I had a bad year," he said at a press conference at the club's Fifth Ave. offices.

"Every ball player has a poor season once in a while, so I guess it was just one of those things. Anyway, I can't afford two bad years in a row and I'm looking forward to a good one."

Yogi's .294 lifetime batting average dropped to .290 when he batted only .251. He did keep up his homer pace with 24, and his lifetime total of 262 is the most ever by a catcher. His RBI mark dropped off to 82 after four straight years of 100 or more. He had 105 in 1956.

BERRA IS THE first Yankee to sign, and the fact that he took a cut could denote a trend. MacPhail admitted as much. It is obvious that men like Tommy Byrne, Don Larsen, Andy Carey, and Whitey Ford are in for slices to compensate for raises to such as Gil McDougald, Hank Bauer, Tony Kubek, Tom Sturdivant, Bob Turley, and, of course, Mickey Mantle.

The cut didn't ruffle Yogi, who has other ventures going for him and is in a high tax bracket, anyway. He and Phil Rizzuto will open their new bowling alley on Route S-3 at Clifton, N.J., either on Feb. 21 or March 1.

Yogi Berra slices a piece of cake in the club office after taking a slice in salary for the first time in 12 years with the Bombers. The backstop will receive about $58,000, a cut of $2,500 from 1957. Berra is the first Yank to sign. (News photo by Gordon Rynders.)

BERRA IS 33 and it is obvious that the Yankees feel he may be slipping. They sent him to the Mayo Clinic for a thorough checkup in December. The doctors reported him in good shape and advised against surgery on his nose, which was broken by a foul tip that smashed his mask in Cleveland last June. Larry Raines tipped the ball, and the aluminum alloy bar split, piercing Berra's beak.

"They [the Mayo medics] said I should see how I breathe in spring training," he said. "But they said the nose should be okay. I feel fine and am going to Florida on the fifth of February to play in the ball players' golf tournament in Miami." ■

Yanks catcher Yogi Berra signs a contract at the Yankee front office as personnel director Lee MacPhail adjusts a new cap for him. (News photo by Gordon Rynders.)

THE POWERHOUSE
by Jimmy Powers

February 14, 1958—This was before the current baseball players' golf tournament had gotten under way and Lawrence Peter Berra was on the practice green. Yogi gave the writer a few putting tips, or, to quote his own tribute to his onetime instructor, Bill Dickey, he "learned me all his experience."

What about the AL race?

"I think we'll win all right but you will see some surprises. I look for Baltimore to be the sleeper club. They could give everyone a lot of trouble."

Speaking of trouble, was Yogi worried about his hitting slump?

"Naturally, you lie awake and wonder what you're doing wrong. I get tips in the mail from plumbers and characters who have never had a bat in their hands. They mean well. And other ball players come up and tell me to try this or try that. It happens to every guy who isn't hittin' normal."

Everyone in baseball is fond of Yogi. He is kidded unmercifully but he takes the riding in rare good humor. He just grins and lets the needles skid off his hide. But he is far from a clown. When you ask about Yankee plans for the infield, for instance, he comes up with the adroit answer . . . "I don't want to say nothin' because after I was interviewed once Casey came to town and he said, 'Guess I got here just in time to save my job. I been readin' the papers and see where Yogi is givin' statements to the press almost like he was the manager.'"

Yogi is a bit more subdued this year. He isn't the comic-book, TV detective serial and gangster movie type he has been painted . . . "Some of those wisecracks they credited to me I never heard of before. I still didn't understand 'em when I read 'em."

Yogi has turned into an efficient, well-dressed, well-spoken business man. Off season he is doing effective work for a soft drink concern. He has several retail businesses going for him and he regularly has to turn down offers to come into still more . . . "I'm concentrating on baseball. I owe everything to the game. I was tickled to death to play for $90 a month in my first job."

June 10, 1958

Berra Batting .221 for Yanks—and 300 in Bowling Lanes

by Dick Young

Yogi Wisdom

"Only in America," Yogi exclaimed when he learned that the mayor of Dublin, Ireland was Jewish.

"It's One, Two, Three Strikes, You Hope, at the Old Bowling Game."

That's Yogi Berra's parodied theme now that he has become a two-sport man by opening a 40-lane bowling palace. The snazzy no-post palace, complete with automatic pinsetters and two bars, is located in a busy shopping center off a highway near Clifton, N.J., and it is there that Yogi spends his spare time, now that golf is taboo under Yankee directive during the season.

Yogi is partners with Phil Rizzuto, his ex-teammate, who now shares the Yankees' play-by-play mikes with Mel Allen and Red Barber. Phil and Yogi have poured more than $50,000 each of their own dough into the place. They rent the building, and have bought, on time, almost $500,000 worth of equipment. That's some charge plate.

"Those pinsetters cost $7,700 apiece," says Yogi proudly, "and each alley costs $3,500."

How is it paid off? Does the manufacturing outfit cut in for 10 cents or so on every line bowled?

"Not this outfit," said Yogi. "We bought the machines from Brunswick, outright, and we make payments. Except they don't make us make payments now; not during the four slow months."

He counted on his fingers … "May … June … July … August" … and said: "Yeah, those are the four months. We start paying again in September, when the busy season starts."

Yogi Berra checks over 40 alleys at his new bowling establishment. Yogi and Phil Rizzuto say they have invested over $50,000 each in the place, which has a bit of a Yankee Stadium motif, with a glass-encased trophy panel containing baseball gloves and MVP awards. (News photo by Joe Petrella.)

Berra intends to keep the place open around the clock when the bowling leagues begin operating. "We'll see how it goes," he said expectantly. "Even now, on weekends, you gotta wait for an alley a lot of times."

The Yankees catcher, three times MVP, applies the baseball motif to his bowling alley's decor. Even the huge bar is shaped like Yankee Stadium. "We call it the Stadium Lounge," beams Yogi.

And the quick-snack room is "The Dugout." The paper place mats are illustrated with an aerial view of Yankee Stadium, and spotted with the upcoming dates of Yankee home games, a month at a time. "We change them every month," Yogi explained.

Near the broad entrance, a glass-encased trophy case on the wall bears numerous Rizzuto and Berra trophies—the three MVP plaques won by Yogi, and the one Rizzuto received.

Yogi pointed out the bronzed beat-up catcher's mitt on the lower shelf. "That's the one I caught two no-hit games with," he said. "You know; Reynolds."

He looked out the glass-panel door toward the vast parking area. "We got enough of it, ain't we?" he said.

Looks that way; how many cars does it handle?

"I don't know," said Yogi with a shrug.

But he'll know how much dough comes in at the end of the month. Your children should be so dumb. ∎

Yogi tries his hand at polishing pins in the alley workshop. (News photo by Joe Petrella.)

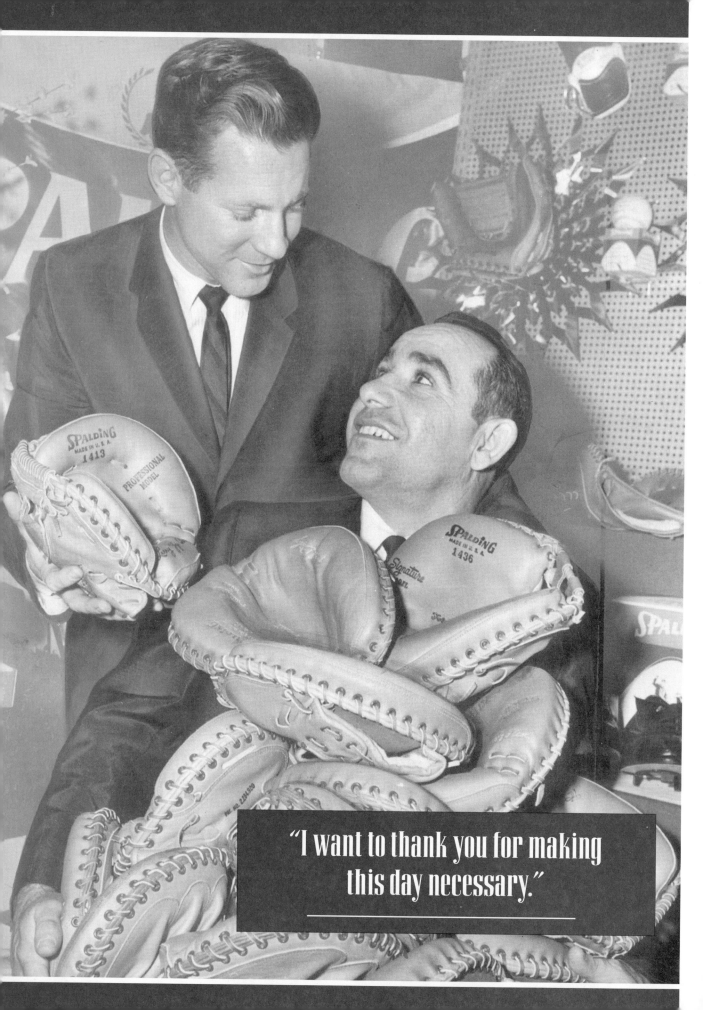

"I want to thank you for making this day necessary."

8

1959: Yogi Day

	G	AB	R	H	2B	3B	HR	RBI	BB	SB	BA	SA
1959:	131	472	64	134	25	1	19	69	43	1	.284	.462

Always a favorite with fans, Yogi seemed to grow more popular every year. In 1959, his thirteenth full season in the majors, Yogi was honored with Yogi Day, celebrated at Yankee Stadium on September 19. Yogi's fans and friends showered the Yankee catcher and his family with gifts, and were rewarded with an emotional speech by the man known for his humor. Yogi was joined at the Stadium by his wife, Carmen, his sons Larry and Timmy, and his father, Pietro.

In addition to being honored at Yogi Day, Berra received the CYO Most Popular Yankee Award for the second time. He was given a jacket from Vermont Governor Robert Stafford during Vermont Day ceremonies at Yankee Stadium in August.

Yogi batted .284 for the season and had 19 home runs. On August 9, he joined the "300" home run club with a game-tying, ninth-inning blast against Kansas City. ■

Dale Berra, 2¹/₂ years old, helps his dad, Yankee catcher Yogi Berra, pack up at the Stadium after the end of the season. (News photo by Pat Candido.)

Yogi 'Chokes' Up Finally— As Fans Give Him 'Day'

by Joe Trimble

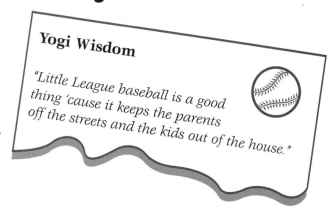

Yogi Wisdom

"Little League baseball is a good thing 'cause it keeps the parents off the streets and the kids out of the house."

The fans and friends of Yogi Berra wished the popular Yankee "buon fortuno" yesterday on his "day" at the Stadium. The veteran catcher was inundated with a truckload of gifts totaling thousands of dollars for himself and his family. There were 58 separate presents in all.

In addition, a $4,000 scholarship in Berra's name at Columbia was awarded to 19-year-old Jim Clevin, top student and athlete and president of the senior class at Lynbrook L.I. High. This was realized from contributions made by the public for Berra Day. The gifts were from merchants and friends and none were purchased from money sent in by fans.

Berra had asked that he receive nothing because he needs nothing. He choked up and cried as he made a speech of acceptance.

"Everything up until now has been fine," he said, starting out with a light manner. "I was enjoying myself and hope you are, too. On behalf of myself and family, I want to thank you . . . not for the gifts but for showing up."

Then, his voice breaking, this humble man went on. "I'm grateful to the wonderful organization, the Yankees, and to my many friends. God bless you all."

He finished in tears, stepped back from the microphone, and stood shyly.

Mel Allen, the master of ceremonies, then called for a standing ovation for the squat man, who helped the Yankees win 10 pennants in his 13 years here.

Yogi Berra waves to the fans as his wife, Carmen, his children Larry, 9, and Timmy, 7, and his father Pietro, join him during ceremonies honoring the Yankee catcher. Yogi was only the sixth Bronx Bomber to be feted with a day. (News photo by Seymour Wally.)

Casey Stengel also spoke, briefly and sincerely. "Ladies and gentleman and children of New York and the United States," he said. "In my 10 years, outside of DiMaggio, the man at the plate, Berra, is the greatest player I ever had to manage, which is a great thing to enhance my career."

DiMag, who served as cochairman with Allen, had been cheered when he took a bow earlier. So had Ted Williams, who presented Berra with golf and fishing equipment on behalf of the Red Sox.

Among the gifts were a swimming pool, a set of redwood outdoor furniture, trips to Italy and Bermuda by air, a color TV set, furniture, a pool table, cosmetics for his wife, Carmen, dance lessons, and a station wagon, the last given by the Yankees management.

The New York sports fotogs pulled a switch by giving the player an autographed baseball, and the baseball writers contributed a silver tray. ■

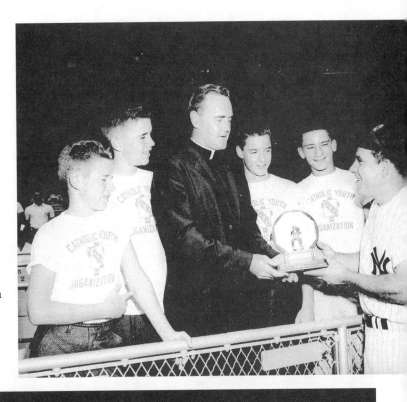

BY POPULAR DEMAND. Father Philip Murphy presents the CYO Most Popular Yankee Award to Yogi Berra as club members look on at the Stadium. It marked the second time the popular Yankee catcher copped the award. (News photo by Charles Hoff.)

SYRUPY REMARKS. Yogi Berra gets a jacket from Vermont's Gov. Robert Stafford during Vermont Day ceremonies at the Stadium. Gil McDougald holds a blanket given to him. Looking on are Vermont's Sen. George Aiken (next to Gil) and Michael O'Shea (l.), representing New York City. (News photo by Charles Hoff.)

January 29, 1959—
Yogi Berra ponders a
new contract as he
waits in the Yankee
office, at 745 Fifth
Ave., to huddle with
the Yankee brass.
There has been a lot of
talk about Yankee pay
cuts. Despite that, he
came out with a bigger
smile, having signed
for $58,000, the same
as he earned last year.
(News photo by Hal
Mathewson.)

August 9, 1959—Yogi
Berra joined the "300"
home run club when
he tied the game in the
9th inning, and Elston
Howard won it with his
homer in the 11th.
(News photo by
Charles Hoff.)

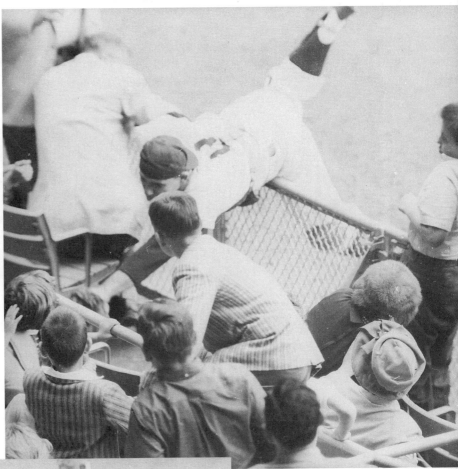

September 21, 1959—Yanks' Yogi Berra dives into the stands going after a foul hit by Boston's Jensen at the Stadium. But the ball kept right on going and so did Berra. (News photo by Dan Farrell.)

Berra's practically hand-standing in the grandstand in a vain try for the catch. (News Photo by Dan Farrell.)

DAILY NEWS

NEW YORK'S PICTURE NEWSPAPER ®

FINAL

5¢

Vol. 42, No. 95   New York 17, N.Y., Friday, October 14, 1960

WEATHER: Some cloudiness, mild.

GOING, GONE!
BUCS CHAMPS

Mazeroski HR Beats Yanks, 10-9

"The other teams could make trouble for us if they win."

9

1960: Heartbreak

	G	AB	R	H	2B	3B	HR	RBI	BB	SB	BA	SA
1960:	120	359	46	99	14	1	15	62	38	2	.276	.446

A s Yogi's playing career began to wind down, he and the Yankees prolonged it by gradually shifting him to the outfield, sparing him the physical strain of catching. The switch began in 1960, when Yogi substituted for an injured Roger Maris in right field. When Maris returned to the lineup, Stengel moved Yogi to left rather than disturb Elston Howard, who had begun to blossom as a full-time catcher.

Left field was where Bill Mazeroski's famous World Series home run found Yogi, as it sailed overhead into the stands in left-center. Mazeroski's Game 7 blast broke a 9-9 tie and gave the Pittsburgh Pirates the 1960 World Championship. Berra, who hit .318 with one home run and eight RBIs during the Series, came into the Fall Classic as the Pirates' "most-feared Yankee," but even he was unable to prevent Mazeroski's 11th-hour heroics. ■

Despite the heartbreak of Mazeroski's homer, Yogi was still smiling as he packed his locker after the 1960 World Series.

October 14, 1960

Bucs Win in the 9th on Maz' HR, 10-9

by Dick Young

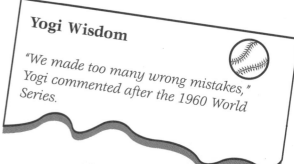

Yogi Wisdom

"We made too many wrong mistakes," Yogi commented after the 1960 World Series.

Great is a tired word. But great, great, great is the only word to describe the ballgame that today made the incredibly Cinderella-ish Pirates the 1960 champions of the baseball world. They won it, 10-9, by outblasting the power-happy Yanks at their own game. They won it on a homer by Bill Mazeroski, first man up in the bottom of the ninth in this seventh, and great, game. They won it on a homer by Hal Smith an inning earlier, when the Pitts came from behind with five runs to take a lead that was to be wiped out in the Yankee ninth.

BY VIRTUE OF THAT spectacular five-run rally, the Bucs led 9-7 going into the ninth inning, and were counting the money—the winners' share, which so many Yankee teams have grown accustomed to counting. But there is inherent class in the Yanks, and it shows to the end.

Richardson led the ninth with a bloop hit to left-center. Dale Long, swinging for DeMawstri, lined another single to right, and just that quickly, reliever Bob Friend was gone.

Now it was Haddix, the smallish southpaw who had won game 5. Haddix was all that was left to Murtaugh, except for the dregs, the sparring partners whom the Yanks had punished so severely and so consistently in games past. It was up to Haddix, or all was lost.

HARVEY HAD SOME tough bats coming up— Maris . . . Mantle . . . Berra . . . Skowron. He jammed Maris' fists, and got him to pop up. But Mantle, swinging righty, is tougher. Mick lashed a curling liner into right for a single. One run was in. The tying run was on third with one out.

Then came the screwiest play of the game—of the series. Berra buzzed a low liner just inside first base. Rocky Nelson, who had skipped off the bag with Mantle on the pitch, leaned back and made a snappy cross-gloved pickup, stepping on first in one motion.

MANTLE, TWO STRIDES farther off the bag than Nelson, turned to see the trap and stood there, transfixed, for a split second. Nelson, his back toward Mantle as he stepped on the bag, anticipated that Mickey would be running toward second. Rock whirled and cocked his arm, as if to fire there for the "reverse DP." Then, he too froze. There they stood, in a strange tableau, staring at each other, no more than 10 feet apart, as though saying: "Whose move?"

BOB'S WIRES

Mayor Wagner sent the following telegrams to Pittsburgh Mayor George Barr and Yank manager Casey Stengel upon the completion of the World Series yesterday.

To Mayor Barr: "Congratulations to the city of Pittsburgh from New York City on the Pirates winning the World Series. A great team defeated a great New York team, but just wait until next year."

To Stengel: "Our city still solidly behind you and hope you will stay with the Yankees and win the Series next year. Congratulations on a great fight. Best wishes to all the Yankees. New York is proud of them."

Along with his wife, Carmen, Yogi's postseason travel plans include a World Series stop in Pittsburgh. (News photo by Frank Hurley.)

They moved simultaneously, and toward each other—Mickey diving headfirst for the bag; Nelson bending over for the tag. In an instinctive, catlike reflex, Mantle went under and around Nelson's outstretched fist and grabbed the bag with his hand—"safe."

IT WAS A TREMENDOUS slide—and a game-saver. Had Nelson made the DP, this game and the Series would have been over at that instant, for pinch runner McDougald still was several steps from home. Instead, Gil crossed and the score was tied.

The third out eventually came on Skowron's grounder, and up for the last of the ninth came the Pirates to face Terry. Ralph threw two pitches to leadoff man Mazeroski. The first was a ball. The second was gone. It flew high and far, over the brick wall in left-center, with left fielder Berra watching it, hopelessly, helplessly.

AROUND THE BASES flew Maz, whirling his right arm in boyish glee. As he rounded third, the fans burst from the lower stands to engulf him. He forced his way through to the plate, and was swallowed up in the seething mass of people and teammates. The cops and state troopers came to rescue him, lest he be torn apart by love.

JOY IS RAMPANT—and there is a minority sadness, too. There are those who wanted Casey Stengel to go out on top. Instead, in his 50th year of baseball, and 70th year of life, he winds up next to the top. Still, as Yankee manager, he has won seven World Series in 12 years, and lost only three. The three he lost were carried to seven games.

He need not apologize. ∎

BUCS FEAR BERRA

by Dick Young

October 4, 1960—The Pirates today beat the tar out of the Yanks—in their pre-Series clubhouse meeting. They knew just how to pitch to every Yank slugger; exactly what every Yank pitcher was going to throw; which Yank outfielders to run on. The Yanks didn't have a chance.

And who do you think is the one man who gave the Bucs trouble—the one they most fear? Not Mickey Mantle, who led the AL in homers. Not Roger Maris, who led the AL in runs batted in. It was none other than the man songs are written about, "Yogi, Baby"—the man who led both leagues in malaprops.

Berra, it was learned after the highly classified meeting, is the name circled, asterisked, and underlined on the scouting reports submitted by Howie Haak and George Detore. He is the most feared Yankee.

Manager Danny Murtaugh admitted as much when questioned by newsmen after the meeting. "Not only our scouts think so," said Murtaugh, "but everybody seems to think Yogi is the man to watch in that certain spot. What was it Paul Richards said? In the last three innings, Berra is the toughest man in baseball."

October 14, 1960

Kubek Goes to Hospital From Costly Bad Hop

by Jim McCulley and Joe Trimble

Pittsburgh, Oct. 13—Tony Kubek couldn't talk after the injury to his larynx today and was taken to a hospital for examination and observation. The brutally bad hop, which felled the Yankee shortstop and cost the Yanks the World Series, caused internal bleeding.

"Don't even try to talk," Dr. Sidney Gaynor advised the 25-year-old infielder after Tony showered and dressed. Kubek nodded and said hoarsely: "Okay."

Gaynor summoned Dr. Henry Sherman, a nose and throat specialist, immediately after the eighth-inning injury. The physicians wanted him to go to the hospital right away but the player insisted on staying until the game was over. He saw the end on a TV set just outside the Yankee dressing room. Only then would he shower and dress.

Dr. Gaynor indicated the internal bleeding made it mandatory that he be hospitalized. The risk of having him where emergency treatment couldn't be given, as in an airplane, was too great. ∎

AIDING THE FALLEN KUBEK. As Yankee shortstop Tony Kubek charged a certain double-play grounder in the eighth inning of Game 7, the ball struck a pebble and smashed into Kubek's throat. The bad-hop grounder opened up the floodgates as Pittsburgh scored five runs in the eighth to wipe out the Yanks' 7-4 lead.

Virdon Catch Turning Point of First Game, Claims Murtaugh

by Jim McCulley

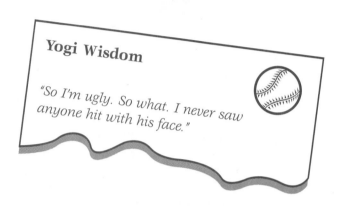

Yogi Wisdom

"So I'm ugly. So what. I never saw anyone hit with his face."

Historic Forbes Field, battleground of so many Hall of Fame ball players, was full of Pirate heroes in today's World Series opener, but the play that stuck out in the mind of winning manager Danny Murtaugh was Bill Virdon's grab of Yogi Berra's bid for an extra-base wallop in the fourth inning.

"Virdon's catch was the turning point in the game for us, without any question," Murtaugh said. "It enabled Law to get out of the inning with a minimum of damage and we pulled away right after that."

THIS POSTGAME interview in Murtaugh's office was something of a first in modern WS history. The opposing manger, Casey Stengel, was sitting right next to the home-team pilot all the while it was going on. Clubhouse conditions made this a necessary convenience for the reporters. In fact, Casey lent an aside or two that livened up the proceedings.

While discussing strategic moves, Murtaugh turned to the Yankee manager, who had been ominously quiet up to that time, and said: "You're not listening to all this, are you, Casey?"

STENGEL BROKE into a grin and answered: "Danny, all you have to do is change things around tomorrow. That'll satisfy me." ■

Yankee sluggers Roger Maris, Yogi Berra, Mickey Mantle, and Moose Skowron powered the club to the 1960 World Series in Casey Stengel's final season as the Yankees' manager.

January 29, 1960

Yogi In at 58G, Has 5-yr. Plan

by Dick Young

Yogi Berra, a living doll considering how he looks, yesterday signed his 14th Yankee contract and revealed his plans and hopes. He wants to catch for five more years or so, on a diminishing basis, then to become a Yankee coach "for the rest of my life, if they'd have me."

Berra is making a repeat $58,000 for the 1960 season. That's an educated guess. His reply to the prying question was: "I'm plenty satisfied. I never thought I'd be making this much money."

He will be 33 in May—and he's still the first-string catcher, ahead of a catcher who'd be No. 1 on almost any other club, Ellie Howard. Yogi was in 131 games, 115 as a catcher, the rest as a pinch hitter or right fielder. He batted .284—18 points better than his previous season, but his homers dropped off to 19, and his RBI to 69. Manager Casey Stengel concedes that the low RBI figure is due to the neglect of other Yankees, who forget to get on base in front of him.

The way Yogi peers into the future, he should be able to catch 100 or so games for the next year, then grade it down to about 70 thereafter; half a season for half pay of, say, $30,000. In addition, he would be a valuable pinch hitter the rest of the time.

Looking the other way, backward, Berra thinks the Yankees blew the pennant last season because "it was just one of those years; nobody did nothing."

Asking to expand the thought, Berra said: "We were plain lousy. Usually we have had one or two guys who'd always pick the club up; this time we didn't."

About the 1960 season, Yogi says: "I think we have a good chance. It all depends on what those young pitchers will do for us"—meaning Jim Coates and Bill Short. About the standbys, Yogi added: "Whitey [Ford] is always good for 16 or 17, and Turley's gotta be better." ∎

Yankee GM George Weiss (l.) and Yogi Berra are all smiles after Yogi inks another contract with the Yankees.

Talk of travel led to Yogi's recent trip to Europe. Berra mentioned that he and his wife visited the Louvre. "Did you like it?" he was asked. "It's all right," said Berra, "if you like paintings."

April 29, 1960

Yogi Next Left-Field Tenant

by Joe Trimble

Now, it's Yogi Berra who is going to occupy Yankee Stadium's left field, otherwise known as "Hell's Half Acre." This sounds like a helluva way to treat an old and faithful retainer, but Casey Stengel has to solve the problem.

"What would you do, now that Maris is ready to play?" the manager asked yesterday after sending the team through a noon workout. Roger Maris, the right fielder, is due back tonight in Baltimore. He has been nursing a sore shin and a puffed ankle for almost a week.

"Play him in left field," was the answer.

"No, he's shown me he is an excellent right fielder and he's gonna stay there. I don't want to get him upset by moving him around."

It was then suggested that Berra, who has been playing right field during Maris' convalescence, be permitted to put on the mask and send Elston Howard to left field.

"NO, I DON'T wanna disturb Howard, either," said the manager. "I've won five games with him catching. He's catching very fine baseball. But what's the matter with Berra playing left field? He says he has played there. I believe he can do it."

Not that Berra has volunteered, you understand. Nobody wants the damned spot, which has befuddled regular outfielders as well as such convertibles as Berra, Howard, and Hector Lopez. The latter was handed the job at the start of the season but lost it with two goofer plays against Boston Tuesday.

STENGEL CONTINUED: "Hunt's a professional outfielder. They tell me he was a good one in the minors. And look what happened to him out there [LF at the Stadium]."

Casey tried Ken Hunt, the rookie, out there Wednesday against Washington, but he lost two flies hit by catcher Earl Battey before Whitey Ford completed his own destruction by throwing a home-run ball to Jim Lemon.

That left-field area is brutal. It is hard to see the ball due to glare, haze, sun, and white shirts when there are people in the third deck. You can't play it by ear, either, because the acoustics fool you.

"EVERY BALL seems to be hit a mile, by the sound of the bat," Hunt says. "Even a broken-bat hit sounds like a good crack. When a batter takes a full cut you think the ball is hit hard by the sound."

Lopez undoubtedly will get the job back because Berra can't play every day. For the time being, Stengel wants to keep the heat off Hector, fearing a psychological problem such as haunted poor Norm Siebern to distraction and eventually moved him on to Kansas City. ∎

Yogi Berra makes a three-point landing after snagging a short fly ball.

"It gets late early out here."

10

1961-62: Returning to the Outfield

	G	AB	R	H	2B	3B	HR	RBI	BB	SB	BA	SA
1961:	119	395	62	107	11	0	22	61	35	2	.271	.466
1962:	86	232	25	52	8	0	10	35	24	0	.224	.388

Although he still spent an occasional game behind the plate, Yogi considered his move to the outfield permanent in 1961, thereby postponing his retirement. In the 1961 World Series against the Cincinnati Reds, Yogi missed the final game because of an injured shoulder, but still managed to collect a number of Series records, breaking nine and tying two. Among his new records were most World Series played (12), most Series games played (72), and most Series hits (71). The Yankees beat the Reds in five games to win their 19th World Championship.

Although his starts began to taper off in 1962, Yogi remained as popular as ever. In January, he and Kyle Rote of the NFL's New York Giants received awards from the New York Press Photographers' Association. On June 9, 1962, Yogi reached yet another milestone, playing in his 2,000th game. The 1962 season also saw another Yankee championship when the Bronx Bombers defeated the San Francisco Giants in seven games. ∎

Right fielder Yogi Berra—that's right, Yogi Berra—gloves a fly ball hit by KC catcher Frank House for the third out in the second inning of the first game. (News photo by Charles Hoff.)

June 13, 1961

Yogi Gets His Wish; He's in Outfield for Good

by Joe Trimble

They made jokes about Yogi Berra, but he knows baseball, and knows what's good for Yogi Berra. "I told you," he said just before last night's home-stand windup against Los Angeles, "that I would hit better if I played the outfield—and last longer, too."

Manager Ralph Houk, who has been playing the Yog in left, agrees emphatically, and adds: "I'm going to try to keep him out there."

Thus, except for an occasional return to the mask in a pinch, the catching career of L. Berra, which has covered 11 World Series, 10 All-Star Games, and a touch of greatness, could be ended. It's to be outfielder Berra from now on.

"The crouching up and down that a catcher has to do tires a man of his age [36]," says Houk. "He keeps his pep longer in the outfield and seems to be a better hitter."

A comparison of statistics confirms the opinion. Going into last night's game, the breakdown of Yogi's double life read:

	AB	H	HR	RBI	BA
OF	81	25	8	16	.296
C	51	14	2	8	.255

Yogi's fielding might be termed "adequate." He is no Mantle or Maris, but how many are? Occasionally, Berra takes a wrong turn or two under a ball hit over his head, but that has happened to better men in the tricky haze of the Stadium's background, as viewed by left fielders. ■

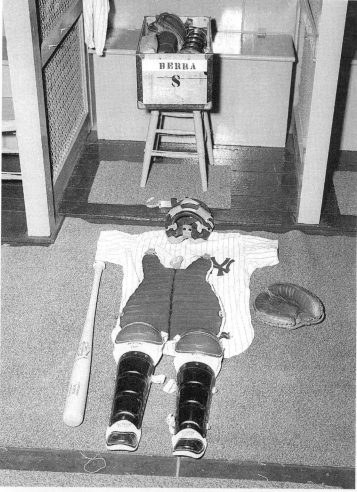

Yogi puts his "tools of ignorance" behind him as he prepares for his move to the outfield. (News photo by Seymour Wally.)

October 7, 1961

Cincy's Glaring Sun Has Yogi in Stew

by Joe Trimble

Cincinnati—If there isn't a song called "Sunlight and Shadows," there should be. For Yogi Berra, who is enduring his first World Series strictly as a left fielder, it may be a dirge. The Yog took his first workout in Crosley Field today and moaned: "It ain't the hill I'm worrying about, it's the sun."

In Yankee Stadium in the second game, he "shadowboxed" a liner into a three-base error which led to a run. Here there are no shadows, just a brutally strong sun and a hill which inclines six feet within 30 feet of the left-field wall.

Usually, the first thing Berra picks up on a field is a bat. Today, he grabbed his glove and dashed out to left field as soon as the workout started. Coach Wally Moses began to hit flies and line drives and Berra, wearing dark glasses like a mendicant in Miami, pawed and clawed at the balls.

"It is rough out here," he said, showing much more concern than his usual lighthearted approach to baseball permits. "The hill keeps you thinking. The wall is hard [concrete] and the balls come off of it fast. And that [censored] sun is the worst of all."

"Here," he said, proffering his glasses to the writer. "Look at it, even through the glasses. You can't hardly see, can you?"

Crosley Field is set in a hollow right in town and the sun beats it from all sides. In most ball parks, there is a definite sun field, either left or right. Here all three fields are sun fields, but left is the worst. ∎

Yogi Berra gets accustomed to Crosley's left-field sun during a workout.

October 5, 1961—At Yankee Stadium in Game 2 of the 1961 World Series, Yogi Berra's two-run homer tied Cincinnati, 2-2. Greeting Yogi at the plate are John Blanchard (38), the on-deck batter; Roger Maris, who scored ahead of Berra; and the batboy. The Reds rallied to win 6-2, for their only Series victory.

"Don't know. They were wearing a bag over their head," Yogi replied when asked whether the streaker he saw was male or female.

Jump Threat

Cincinnati—The Yankee workout at Crosley Field was interrupted today when a naked man threatened for about 15 minutes to jump off a 75-foot-high elevator shaft which runs up the side of the ball park. The man was finally coaxed from his perch by a friend.

Police described the would-be jumper as a man who liked to hang around the park and had occasionally worked out with the Reds. The police said the man apparently had not been drinking.

October 10, 1961

Yanks (by Hec!) Take It, 13-5, in Five

Blanchard and Co. Give Eight Red Hurlers the Biz

by Dick Young

Cincinnati—The Yanks won everything today, including the 13-run pool. They won the game, 13-5. They won the 1961 World Series, 4 games to 1. And they won the shuddering respect of the Cincinnati fans with a fearsome power display that required the record use of eight pitchers by Cincy's miseried manager, Fred Hutchinson.

This is the first time a "B-squad" clinched a World Series. Mickey Mantle was out with his aching rump. So was Yogi Berra, who yesterday injured his right shoulder in a slide. So in the realigned Yankee outfield, Johnny Blanchard played right and Hector Lopez left. And who did most of the ball-bleeding? Hector Lopez and Johnny Blanchard.

Houk, too, had more than distinguished himself. He, the successor to the great Casey Stengel, was the man on the spot. Houk came through by winning a World Championship in his rookie year. Only Bucky Harris (Washington, 1924) and Ed Dyer (Cardinals '46) had done it before.

Now, they no longer say Houk is on the spot. Now they say: "Anyone can manage the Yankees." ∎

Record Harvest for Yogi: Breaks 9 and Equals 2

Cincinnati—Yogi Berra, as expected, reaped the largest harvest of records in the 1961 World Series. The squat Yankee slugger broke nine records and equaled two, although he was forced to sit out today's final game because of an injured right shoulder.

Among the major records Berra set for total Series performances were most Series played (12), most games played (72), most hits (71), most singles (49), and most runs batted in (39). He also equaled marks for most times member of winning club as active player (9) and most long hits for total Series (22).

Bobby Richardson of the Yankees equaled three records for a five-game Series—most at-bats (23), most hits (9), and most singles (8). Teammate John Blanchard equaled two records for a five-game Series—most home runs (2) and most extra bases on long hits (7).

∎ PHONE FACTS ∎

The New York Telephone Company reported yesterday that for the first four days of the World Series, 279,486 telephone calls for scores were made to its time bureau, Meridian 7-1212. A spokesman said the figure was arrived at by subtracting the normal number of calls for the four days from the total.

YOGI IN LEFT TO LIVEN YANKS

by Jim McCulley

June 6, 1962—It will be head-and-head for first place in the American League when the Yankees and Indians square off today at the Stadium in the opener of a series that was curtailed to a pair of games by yesterday's rain.

When the Bombers take the field this afternoon, Yogi Berra will be back in left field. That's the only lineup change Ralph Houk will make at the beginning of this 10-game home stand, and it is highly significant.

Since the Bombers lost Mickey Mantle because of a leg injury, they have lacked a leader in the field. That's the primary reason Houk wants Yogi back in the lineup.

"Yogi still has a big bat. He's a player who has to play to be at his best and I'm going to play him," said Houk yesterday. "He hasn't been doing much as a pinch hitter. But he still commands a lot of respect from the pitchers and I think the club will go better with Yogi in the lineup.

"From now on until further notice, Berra is going to play left field," said the manager.

Even against left-handers?, Houk was asked.

"That never made any difference to Berra," said Houk, "when he's swinging right. And I think he's beginning to get back in the groove."

Yogi has not been contented on the bench while Pepitone and Lopez have been playing left field. He doesn't believe he's through as a regular.

"I wouldn't be here if I didn't think I could help the club," he has said time and again.

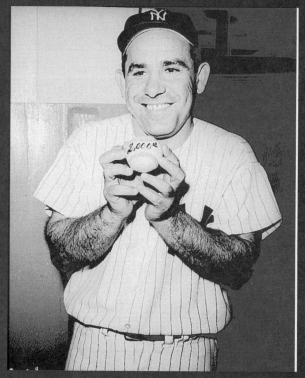

June 9, 1962—Yogi with a ball from his 2,000th game. He also won the game with a homer. (Photo by Walter Kelleher.)

Don Did It

October 9, 1962—Someone approached the Giants' Don Larsen the day before Sunday's World Series game against the Yankees and said:

"Tomorrow is an important anniversary."

"Yes, I know," said the man who, on October 8, 1956, pitched a perfect World Series game against the Dodgers at Yankee Stadium.

"Too bad you're not starting," was the follow-up to Larsen, who has become strictly a reliever for San Francisco.

"Naw," he said, smiling broadly. "I wouldn't get THEM out."

P.S.: Larsen relieved in the sixth, got one man out with the bags full, and became the winning pitcher.—Young

WORLD SERIES SUMMARY ■

Game 1 at Candlestick Park, San Francisco, Oct. 4

N.Y.	2	0	0	0	0	0	1	2	1	-	6	11	0
S.F.	0	1	1	0	0	0	0	0	0	-	2	10	0

W—Ford; L—O'Dell. HR—Boyer. A.—43,852

Game 2 at Candlestick Park, San Francisco, Oct. 5

N.Y.	0	0	0	0	0	0	0	0	0	-	0	3	1
S.F.	1	0	0	0	0	0	1	0	X	-	2	6	0

W—Sanford; L—Terry. HR—McCovey (SF). A.—43,910

Game 3 at Yankee Stadium, NY, Oct. 7

S.F.	0	0	0	0	0	0	0	0	2	-	2	4	3
N.Y.	0	0	0	0	0	0	3	0	X	-	3	5	1

W—Stafford; L—Pierce. HR—Bailey (SF). A.—71,434

Game 4 at Yankee Stadium, NY, Oct. 8

S.F.	0	2	0	0	0	0	4	0	1	-	7	9	1
N.Y.	0	0	0	0	0	2	0	0	1	-	3	9	1

W—Larsen; L—Coates. HR—Haller (SF), Hiller (SF). A.—66,607

Game 5 at Yankee Stadium, NY, Oct. 10

S.F.	0	0	1	0	1	0	0	0	1	-	3	8	2
N.Y.	0	0	0	1	0	1	0	3	X	-	5	6	0

W—Terry; L—Sanford. HR—Pagan (SF), Tresh (NY). A.—63,165

Game 6 at Candlestick Park, San Francisco, Oct. 15

N.Y.	0	0	0	0	1	0	0	1	0	-	2	3	2
S.F.	0	0	0	3	2	0	0	0	X	-	5	10	1

W—Pierce; L—Ford. HR—Maris (NY). A.—43,948

Game 7 at Candlestick Park, San Francisco, Oct. 16

N.Y.	0	0	0	0	1	0	0	0	0	-	1	7	0
S.F.	0	0	0	0	0	0	0	0	0	-	0	4	1

W—Terry; L—Sanford. A.—43,948

Yanks Bag WS on Terry 4-Hitter, 1-0

Moose Scores in 5th on Double Play; Giants Barely Miss in 9th-Inning Bid

by Dick Young

San Francisco—This most unusual baseball season today ended in the most usual way—with the Yankees world champs. They are champs for the 20th time, because Ralph Terry, the lanky, handsome Oklahoman, snuffed out the Giant power, 1-0, on four hits to put a fitting end to this pitcher-dominated seven-game tournament. This most unusual baseball season had gone 172 games for the weary Giants; three fewer for the Yanks, who drew a bye in the play-off—and here it finally ended, with the title decided by one run.

That run came in the fifth, scored by Moose Skowron, and prodded across by Tony Kubek's double-play grounder with the bags full. The Giants' manager, Al Dark, had decided to play the infield back, perfectly content to settle for one run in that sticky situation—but never dreaming the one run would be all he and the 43,948 fans would see this day.

The fans, disappointed in the result, left with the satisfaction of seeing a tremendous game—a half-bid at a perfect performance by Terry, who retired the first 17 batters. They saw, too, a strong try by Jack Sanford, who was facing Terry for the third time in the Series— a personal rubber match.

Sanford went till the eighth, when the Yanks again loaded the bags with none down, and this time Billy O'Dell came on to strangle the threat with an amazing five-pitch relief gem.

They also saw a stomach bubbling Giant challenge to tie in the ninth, or perhaps to win. Matty Alou, batting for O'Dell, led with a perfect drag bunt to the right side. He marked time while Terry fanned brother Felipe and Chuck Hiller—leaving it up to

Willie Mays with one out left. Mays sliced a streamer into the right corner for a double, and the speedy Matty Alou streaked for third. He rounded the base as the Maris-Richardson relay came in strong.

Coach Whitey Lockman flagged down Alou, who ducked back into third as Richardson's peg took a high hop into Howard's mitt, back of the plate. There are some who think Alou might have beaten the relay. I am not one of them. In fact, he might have been out, big.

So with the tying run on third, the winner on second, up stepped long Willie McCovey, who had tripled his previous time up. Mac got a good piece of the ball this time, too. He laced a low liner toward the right side. Little Bobby Richardson shot his glove up to protect his face, and caressed the ball fondly.

Terry, as though momentarily in shock, did not respond. Then, after staring at Richardson, Ralph tossed his glove with a sighing motion into the air— then flipped his cap after it. His mates pounded him, and hugged him—and eventually Clete Boyer and Bill Stafford carried him off on their shoulders. ■

Winners' Due

October 17, 1962—As soon as the last out was registered in the Series finale in San Francisco yesterday, the staff of examiners in The News' $5,000 World Series contest went to work to determine the prize-winners. At stake was $2,500 for first prize; $1,000 for second; $500 for third; $250 for fourth; and $75 each for fifth to 14th

January 16, 1962—Flashing smiles, Kyle Rote of the Football Giants and Yogi Berra hold plaques given them in 1962 by the New York Press Photographers' Assocation at a dinner at Toots Shor's. Photographers said they are a couple of easy-to-get-along-with guys. (News photo by Bill Quinn.)

October 3, 1962—Yogi looks on as Whitey Ford plants a playful kiss on the cheek of Yogi's wife, Carmen. The Yanks were at the airport preparing to leave for Game 1 of their World Series matchup with the San Francisco Giants. The Yanks captured their 20th World Championship by beating the Giants in the seventh game, 1-0.

"You've got to be careful if you don't know where you're going, because you might not get there."

11

1963-64: The Wild Ride

Perhaps the Beatles were thinking of Yogi's 1964 season when they wrote the lyrics to their hit song "The Long and Winding Road." Yogi ended his playing days after the 1963 season and began 1964 full of optimism as rookie manager for the greatest franchise in sports. But from that point on very little went as planned.

Yogi watched in frustration, then exploded in anger as a divisive midseason slump drove the Yankees toward the middle of the league standings. But Yogi's firm resolve and infectious enthusiasm rallied the club; they went on to win their 29th pennant, clinching the title by one game over the Chicago White Sox on the next-to-last day of the season. Yogi man-

aged through a grueling seven-game World Series, which ended in defeat by the St. Louis Cardinals, and was abruptly fired the next day. But before the World Series cheers had died down, Yogi closed out the year by signing on to help coach the woeful, upstart Mets.

From the most decorated team in baseball to the most laughable, it was indeed a wild ride for Yogi in 1964. And one he never regretted. ∎

January 29, 1964—The new year got off to a great start when Yogi joined Yankee GM Ralph Houk (l.) and Giants player and assistant football coach Andy Robustelli (r.) as recipients of the New York Press Photographers' Association award for the most cooperative sports figures of 1963.

October 25, 1963

Yogi Ends Playing Career, Takes Cut for Pilot's Job

by Joe Trimble

"We are losing a great player, and getting a great manager." With those poignant words, Dan Topping yesterday introduced Yogi Berra to some 100 newsmen and TV cameras. The Yankee prexy, who two days earlier had elevated Ralph Houk to the general managership, went on to explain that Yogi will be a non-playing manager, and that Yogi's one-year contract calls for a cut in salary—which must prove great managers aren't as important as great players.

"The salary," said Topping, "is the same as Stengel and Houk started with as managers here." That would put it at $35,000—an estimated $5,000 slice.

Kidded by the newsmen about the reduction, Yogi said: "It wasn't a big cut," as though he tips caddies that much.

They kept carping on the salary angle, and Berra finally said: "Look, if I do a good job, I'll get more. If I'm not capable of managing, I don't deserve a big salary."

YOGI, UNDER questioning, revealed that:

• He will name his coaching staff in a week or so. (It is likely Frank Crosetti, Johnny Sain, and Jim Hegan will be retained. Possibility for the vacancy created by Yogi's elevation: Gene Woodling.)

• At 38, he is through as a player.

• He believes the Yankees "are gonna be a terrific team"—better than last year.

THE BERRA "batessimo," complete with espresso coffee, was a fun thing. Yogi's natural humor was woven throughout the question-answer session. He handled things well. There were direct answers, some pure wisdom, some hilarious "Berraisms."

On his feelings about the job: "I just hope I can stay in the same shoes as Houk did."

On what he picked up from the managers he had played for: "You can observe a lot just by watching."

SOME OF THE repartee went like this:

HIS JOY'S UNMASKED. Newly named Yank manager Yogi Berra is pictured with his first battery (all mikes) following the announcement at the Savoy Hilton. Yogi, upped to a vacancy created by Ralph Houk's promotion, is taking a cut in salary but, like someone said, he'll manage to get by. (News photo by Charles Hoff.)

Q. What makes a good manager?

A. A good ball club.

Q. What will you do when the general manager comes to the clubhouse to second-guess you?

A. I'll throw him out. [Houk, standing nearby, laughed.]

Q. What do you see as your biggest problem?

A. If I can manage; that's my biggest problem.

Q. DO YOU BELIEVE you can be harsh with the players when the occasion demands?

A. In anything you do, you have to put your foot down somewhere along the line.

Q. Do you believe it will be difficult to break in without the benefit of managerial experience in the minors?

A. I've been up here 17 years, watching games and learning. If I can't manage, I'll quit. If I'm good, I'll stick around a little longer.

IF GOOD WISHES of his players and fans will have any bearing, Berra will be around a lot longer. The squat little man with the attractively homely face is one of the most popular ever to have played ball in New York.

Following the press conference at the Savoy Hilton, Yogi walked to the Waldorf Astoria to make his first public appearance as manager—at the Topps Gum affair, honoring the All-Star rookie team.

As Berra entered the room, some 500 baseball people were on their feet, applauding. Joe Garagiola, Berra's childhood buddy, was emceeing the affair, and invited Yogi to the rostrum to say a few words. The

man who had just been given the most coveted managerial job in baseball went to the mike and said: "What's new?" ■

PILOTS: '03-'64

Griffith	1903-1908
Elberfeld	1908
Stallings	1909
Stallings-Chase	1910
Chase	1911
Wolverton	1912
Chance	1913
Chance-Peckinpaugh	1914
Donovan	1915-1917
Huggins	1918-1929
Shawkey	1930
McCarthy	1931-1945
McCarthy-Dickey-Neun	1946
Harris	1947-1948
Stengel	1949-1960
Houk	1961-1963
Berra	1964

OK With Rog

Roger Maris predicted Yogi Berra would make a good manager for the Yankees. In commenting on the promotion of his teammate, Maris said Berra has "a lot of good qualities and capabilities."

He said he and Berra always got along well together. Maris refused to speculate on whether Berra would be as humorous as a manager as he was as a player. "There's not too much I can say about it," Maris said. "He's my new boss."

November 2, 1963

Yogi Says He's Real Manager, No Puppet

by Jim McCulley

Yogi Wisdom

"I just hope I can stay in the same shoes as Houk did," Yogi replied when asked about his new manager's job.

Yogi Berra says he's going to run the Yankees, although he looks forward to sitting down with general manager Ralph Houk to work things out.

"It's not gonna be like some of the writers think, that Houk is gonna run the club," the newly named manager told a reporter.

"I'LL ASK HIS advice on certain things, of course, but he won't tell me things unless I ask him.

"In fact, it's gonna be a lot of fun, sitting down with Ralph and working things out. You see, he knows the players as well as I do, but he won't dictate to me like some general managers.

"In fact, Ralph and I will get together just as soon as I get back to New York. I'll pick my coaching staff and we'll go over the player roster.

"I'VE WORKED under some good managers—McCarthy, Harris, Stengel, and Houk—and I guess I've picked up a little something from each of them. But I won't pattern myself after anybody. I think everybody has to do things his own way, and that's the way I'll manage."

Berra, in fact, sounded more confident about moving up from player to manager than he did about his week-long stab at golf. He finished with a creditable 86 despite a hook on the 16th hole which brought a grimace and an "oh, dear!" Ladies were present. He'll probably use more colorful language as Yankee manager.

BERRA SAID THE few additions to next year's Yankee club will be a couple of young pitchers.

"I've got my four starters, and you take away Whitey Ford and it's a young staff. I'm hoping for a better year from Bill Stafford—he didn't do much last season—and if he comes around, I'd rather have those young pitchers at Richmond, pitching regularly, where I can grab 'em if I need 'em."

THOUGHTFULLY, HE added: "You know, it would be a miracle if the same things happen that happened to Ralph last season. I just don't see how you could lose your two best ball players—Mickey Mantle and Roger Maris—for most of the season and still win."

But won't Mantle likely follow his pattern and be out part of 1964?

"Yeah, Mick's got that bad leg," Berra replied. "But lemme tell you, that guy plays a lot of times just because he wants to play. He's played plenty of times when he's hurting bad. He's that kind." ■

Yogi has made it clear that he will be running the show as the Yankees' new manager this season. (News photo by Dan Farrell.)

November 10, 1963

Surprise-Choice Yogi on Managerial Spot

by Red Foley

After crouching behind home plate for 17 years, Yogi Berra stood before a battery of microphones, cameras, and grinning newsmen here recently and without once thanking anyone "for making this day necessary," accepted an offer to manage the Yankees in 1964.

What has to be an even bigger surprise than Berra's being named to the position is his admittance that he took a salary cut. This must be the first time in baseball history a player ever took a slice to become a manager.

That the player should be none other than Yogi, whose arithmetic has always been far better than his grammar, is almost as unbelievable as being told Einstein flunked long division.

JUST WHAT BERRA will be paid next season is a matter of conjecture. Only Satchel Paige's true age is a better-kept secret than a ball player's salary.

Dan Topping, who is so rich he can even support ulcers, interrupted Berra's acceptance speech long enough to explain to the roomful of newsmen, most of whom couldn't even afford heartburn, that Yogi was being given the identical salary that both Stengel and Houk received in their first years at the Yankee helm.

It's estimated Yogi will get $35,000 for handing the Yankee lineups to the umps next season. At his peak, Berra's top pay was about $55,000.

The idea of Berra being groomed to replace Houk in the pilothouse was first proposed during the 1962 World Series.

ROY HAMEY TOLD Topping he was contemplating retirement and when they approached Houk to replace Hamey, all three zeroed in on Yogi. Sworn to secrecy since last January, Berra peered over Houk's shoulder all season and not a soul toppled as to what was going on.

Yogi explained the entire scheme, step by step, as he related his ascendancy to Houk's chair. Asked how he thought he'd do as Houk's replacement, Berra said: "I only hope I can stand in Ralph's shoes as good as he did."

Now you know that's not exactly what Yogi meant, but that's the way it came out. The same thing happened when someone else asked if he really learned a lot by watching and studying Houk's managerial moves.

"You can observe a lot just by watching," Yogi said.

It's like his tongue gets in the way of his eyeteeth and he can't see what he's saying.■

How Sweet!

At a press conference, Yogi Berra happened to mention that he had recently marked his wedding anniversary. "What did you get your wife?" a newsman asked.

"Well, you know this is the steel anniversary," said Yogi, "so I bought her some pots and pans."

Yanks Name Ford Pitching Coach in Surprise Switch

by Joe Trimble

In a year of surprises, the Yankees came up with another yesterday when Whitey Ford, dean of the staff, was appointed pitching coach to succeed Johnny Sain. The move was made hurriedly when Sain made contractual demands that the club refused to meet. The super-southpaw will continue as an active pitcher, of course.

As late as Wednesday, when the appointment of first-base coach Jim Gleeson was announced, the Bombers said the other coaches would return. Manager Yogi Berra had talked with Frank Crosetti, Jim Hegan, and Sain by phone and all said they'd be back.

Ford, Berra, and GM Ralph Houk appeared at the hastily called press conference at Shor's yesterday to explain the sudden switch. So did co-owner Dan Topping, who flew to Miami afterward.

Ford was in New Hampshire at a dinner and returned Wednesday night. Yogi called him at his home in Lake Success, Long Island.

"I was so surprised when he brought it up that I didn't know what to say," Whitey explained. "So I handed the phone to Joannie [Mrs. Ford] and told her to talk to Yogi for a few minutes while I cleared my head.

"THEN I GOT BACK on the phone and told him I'd like to think it over and that I'd let him know after sleeping on it. I wanted to be sure I could do two jobs. The mental angle, I mean: pitching every fourth day myself and worrying about the other pitchers the rest of the time. I decided I can do it."

Berra is quite happy. "Nobody knows more about pitching than Whitey," the new manager said, "and he is a good teacher."

Asked if he now would take himself out of games he was pitching, Whitey answered, "No, Yogi will still do that. He's done it for years. When he was catching and started looking toward the bench and shaking his head, I knew I was on my way." ■

Southpaw Whitey Ford is joined by manager Yogi Berra and GM Ralph Houk after being named as the Yankees' pitching coach. Ford will continue to pitch for the Yanks as well and will receive an estimated $60,000 for his double duty.

February 29, 1964

Yogi Promises Yank Vets Easy Spring

by Joe Trimble

Yogi Wisdom

"Good players," Yogi replied when asked what makes a good manager.

Fort Lauderdale—Old ball players are like old dogs—they prefer to take it easy in hot weather. Yogi Berra isn't so far removed from his playing days to forget how much of a chore training can be, so the new Yankee manager has decided on less work for the big boys this spring.

"I'm leaving Mickey entirely on his own," Berra said of Mantle today. "I don't have to play him full games at all when we start the exhibitions. Mantle was hurt in an exhibition here last year.

"And I'd like to give the infielders a rest, too. Kubek and Richardson are strong men physically but they can get tired, too. Pepitone will be rested at times, too. I have Harry Bright who can play first base. In fact, all the regulars will be rested." ■

Yogi Berra finds himself in the position of an armchair manager at Yankee Stadium after yesterday's season opener with Boston was postponed by rain. The game and the debut of Yogi have been rescheduled for today. The Yanks will stay with the same lineup. The opening-day hurlers will be Ford and Monbouquette. (News photo by Bill Meuer.)

Yogi Shrugs Off Opening-Day Loss, Lauds Whitey

by Norm Miller

Yogi Berra manfully and philosophically shrugged off his first defeat as Yankee manager yesterday and allowed he could learn to live with it "just as long as it doesn't happen too often."

"No, I don't feel too badly," he replied in answer to a newsman's question as he sat in the seat once occupied by Casey Stengel and Ralph Houk. "If we play like we did today, we're not going to lose many games."

HE SAT THERE relaxed, readily answered all questions, smiled, and occasionally joked. And he said he was especially pleased with the opening-game performances of Whitey Ford and Mickey Mantle, two of his stars who had been something of question marks in spring training.

"They said Whitey couldn't go more than seven, but here he went 11 strong innings and was tremendous," Yogi remarked. "And they said Mickey couldn't run, but he sure moved pretty fast out there on that soft, wet ground."

HIS LAST observation referred to Mantle's spectacular one-handed running catch that robbed Carl Yastrzemski of a possible triple with a man on base in the ninth.

Someone asked him if he second-guessed himself on any decisions he made during the game.

"No, I don't see any reason why I should second-guess myself," he replied. "I never considered lifting Whitey in the 11th. When I went out there after Bob Tillman's triple, I told him to watch out for the squeeze because [Dick] Williams is a good bunter. But the game was all Whitey's to win or lose." ■

April 16, 1964—The auspicious moment is minutes away as Yogi Berra, debuting as the Yankees' manager, gets a pep talk from the boss, Dan Topping, in the Stadium dugout. The words of inspiration didn't get through to the team, though, as the Bronx Bombers were shot down, 4-3, by the Boston Red Sox. (News photo by Dan Farrell.)

First 14 Weeks Lotsa Fun, but Berra Prefers to Win

by Norm Miller

Yogi Berra looked back yesterday on his first 14 weeks of managing and admitted he never knew it could be this much fun. Not only that, it's bound to get better. The extent to which it does get better, of course, will depend on how fast the Yankees move back into first place and stay there. They're a game and one-half out of first as they open a three-game series against the Senators tonight at the Stadium, with Jim Bouton starting against Washington's Dave Stenhouse.

Yogi laughs these days when he thinks back to his doubts and fears of last winter. He promised himself and the Yankees that if he proved to be a failure, or didn't like managing, he'd quit. It took just one month of the regular season to wipe out all those misgivings.

MANAGING HAS NOT changed Yogi the man. He hasn't lost sleep or growled at his wife and kids after defeat; he didn't panic when the Yankees fell six games off the pace on June 10, and when they were four games out early this month.

He hasn't lost his sense of humor. He enjoys his family, the bantering with writers, his golf on days off, and, most important, he enjoys his ball club.

What does he like most about managing?

"Matching wits with the other managers," he replies. "I enjoy tryin' to outthink 'em."

ASK YOGI ABOUT his proudest move this season and he'll reply without hesitation, "Mikkelsen." He refers, of course, to Pete Mikkelsen, the rookie whom many in the front office wanted to farm out after spring training, but who, Yogi insisted, would make a fine pitcher.

The most valuable asset Yogi brought to his job, he feels, was his many playing seasons with the Yankees. These immunized him against panic, taught him to keep calm and not succumb to desperate moves during losing streaks.

Handling of pitchers, Berra agrees, is the toughest part of a manager's daily decisions. He's been booed on occasion, nearly always for staying one batter too long with a faltering pitcher.

"THE BOOING hasn't bothered me," he said. "We've always been booed on the road. I got to like it after a while. As a player, it made me bear down harder." ∎

WREATHED IN A SMILE. Yogi Berra's draped in a good luck wreath before the opener, marking his debut as a major league manager. (News photo by Dan Farrell.)

August 21, 1964

Discord on Yank Bus

by Joe Trimble

The Yankees, banjo hitters during their costly four straight defeats in Chicago, tried the harmonica late today and it sounded a discordant note when Yogi Berra, showing no appreciation for music, loudly reprimanded Phil Linz for breaking the sullen silence with his mouth organ.

The charter bus, bearing the Bombers from Comiskey Park to O'Hare Airport for the flight here, served as Linz' recital hall. Sitting in the rear, the reserve infielder began tootling.

"SHUT THAT THING UP," roared Berra, sitting in the front. Moments later, Linz' instrument was heard again. Berra, leaping from his chair, advanced toward Linz.

"I told you to stop that thing. You'd think you just won four straight," he bellowed. Linz, a frightened look on his face, flipped the harmonica toward the on-charging manager. Yogi batted it with his open hand, and the edge nicked and cut the right knee of Joe Pepitone, sitting nearby.

"Why are you getting on me?" Linz, still sitting, asked. "I give 100% on the field. I try to win. I should be able to do what I want off the field."

"I'LL TAKE CARE of you," Berra stammered, as he returned to his seat. The manager, who has shown remarkable patience during the club's slump against Baltimore and Chicago, refused to discuss the incident.

Frank Crosetti, sitting nearby, began berating Linz from a distance and the infielder traded shouts with the veteran coach. "This is the worst thing I've seen in 33 years with the club," Crosetti later told newsmen. ∎

Several years later, when Yogi and Phil Linz were reunited with the Mets, Linz playfully reprised his role as the harmonic offender.

August 22, 1964

Yogi Downbeat Costs Phil 200 Notes

by Joe Trimble

Boston—Yogi Berra, playing Two for the Money instead of Name That Tune, fined Phil Linz $200 tonight for the Yankee infielder's harmonica recital on an airport-bound bus in Chicago yesterday. The announcement was made prior to the Yankees' Fenway Park arclighter against the Red Sox and followed a closed-door meeting between Berra and Linz.

"I now consider the incident closed," Berra said after levying his first fine as Yankee manager. Linz, dressed in uniform and with the offending harmonica nowhere in sight, said he apologized for the rumpus and admitted it was entirely his fault.

"Yogi said it's over and I'm glad he feels that way," the 25-year-old Linz said. General manager Ralph Houk, who arrived here earlier today, attended the confab but insisted the action taken was entirely Berra's responsibility.

"I left the matter entirely in Berra's hands," Houk said. "But I will add that I don't approve of playing a harmonica on the bus after losing four straight."

Considering the seriocomic overtones, Berra's levy, to some, may seem too severe. But the manager had to exercise his authority. If not, he risked the chance of fostering further displays of disrespect by his players.

The Yankees have been engulfed in pennant pressure for the past two weeks, and the steam started seeping through. Thus, when Linz broke the sullen silence with his newly acquired harmonica, Berra suddenly lost his "What, me worry?" look.

He loudly berated Linz and wound up his verbal onslaught with an "I'll take care of you" threat. The infielder, stunned somewhat by Yogi's tongue-lashing, was spunky enough to ask: "Why are you getting on me? What have I done? I always give

100% on the field. I try to win, and I should be able to do what I want off the field."

Yankee players were still undecided whether or not Linz' unappreciated recital would help or hinder the club. Some felt it might bind them together in their quest for a fifth straight AL flag while others admitted his open defiance of their manager might drive the team further apart.

At this stage of the season and with the schedule running out on them, the Yankees vitally need harmony and not harmonicas. ∎

Phil Linz' playing days with the Yankees will forever be overshadowed by his harmonica playing.

FAMILY DAY AT YANKEE STADIUM. Everybody—well, almost everybody—is wearing a big smile in the Yankee dugout at the Stadium, where Yogi Berra holds Mickey Boyer. Other kids are the children of Yankees Stan Williams, John Blanchard, Joe Pepitone, and Steve Hamilton. (News photo by Charles Hoff.)

RAIN TRUST. One of the thousand things a manager can do on a rainy day is to go over the rest of the league. Yankee coach Frank Crosetti and manager Yogi Berra review the scouting report during a rain-out at the Stadium.

The majors' newest manager, Yogi Berra, sports a mood of confidence as he gazes out upon his troops. (News photo by Dan Farrell.)

October 4, 1964

Yanks Rally to 5th Straight Pennant

Pop Champagne With 5 in 8th, 8-3

by Joe Trimble

This was the year of the Big Y and the Big Eye in the American League. The Yankees won their 29th pennant and CBS its first in a rousing windup yesterday at the Stadium. The battling Bombers burst loose from a 3-3 tie with five runs in the eighth inning and an 8-3 victory over the Indians.

It was their 99th victory and made Yogi Berra, the lovable gargoyle, a winner in his first year as manager. Now all he has to do is win the World Series to emulate his predecessor, who was the first rookie pilot to win both the pennant and world championship. CBS, which bought the club on August 14, can be the first network to go one for one in the majors.

Yogi was the center of celebration in the champagne-splattered dressing room.

"Believe me," he yelled, "this is the greatest thing that ever happened to me. I hadn't been sleepin' too good the last few nights and I was beginning to worry. After this, nothing will ever bother me!"

Berra was bathed in the bubbly, most of it poured over his balding pate by Phil Linz, the harmonica rascal who had inadvertently helped turn the tide in August when, after the loss of four games in Chicago, he played the mouth organ in the bus en route from Comiskey Park to O'Hare Airport.

The arrival of Mel Stottlemyre in mid-August from Richmond and Pedro Ramos from Cleveland on the Labor Day weekend also helped. Stottlemyre provided a strong arm for the starting staff and won

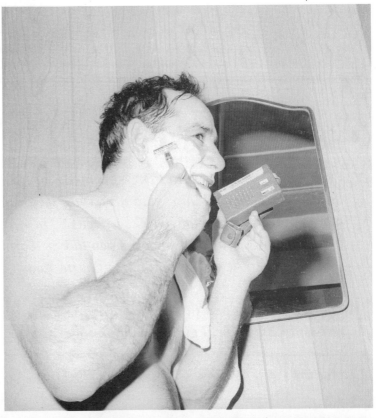

Yogi Berra works up a lather as he listens to news of activities in Comiskey Park while shaving in the Stadium dressing room. The locals had already topped Cleveland, 5-2, to clinch a tie for the AL flag. Meanwhile, the White Sox were taking a pair, 3-2 and 5-4, from the Athletics in the Windy City, to forestall the Yankees' champagne party at the Stadium. Today could be it! (News photo by Dan Farrell.)

nine of 12. Ramos saved the bullpen and it was the Cuban perfecto who nailed down the final three outs yesterday.

The Yankee players roared from the dugout, with Berra leading, and mobbed Ramos in the center of the diamond as the fans unloosened volleys of cheers and reams of torn papers and programs.

This was the second time they've won five AL pennants in succession, a feat no other club has accomplished. They took five in a row from 1949-53, lost in '54, copped four straight before bowing in 1959, and once more have stitched five. The only manager who beat them in 15 years is Al Lopez, and he finished second with the White Sox this time.■

FINAL AMERICAN LEAGUE STANDING OF THE CLUBS

	W.	L.	Pct.	G.B.
YANKEES	99	63	.611	—
Chicago	98	64	.605	1
Baltimore	97	65	.599	2
Detroit	85	77	.525	14
Los Angeles	82	80	.507	17
Minnesota	79	83	.488	20
Cleveland	79	83	.488	20
Boston	72	90	.445	27
Washington	62	100	.383	37
Kansas City	57	105	.352	42

No Kubek

October 4, 1964—Tony Kubek's sprained right wrist may keep him out of the World Series. Dr. Sidney Gaynor said yesterday it is a bad sprain and added: "These things can take from two to four weeks to heal." The Yankee shortstop jammed it sliding into a base at the Stadium two weeks ago today. Gaynor said it might not heal for two more weeks, that progress had been quite slow.

Yogi Berra conceded this was bad news. "We are going to have to ask to have somebody put on in his place, I guess," the manager said.

Meaning Pete Ramos?

"No," he answered. "It can't be a pitcher. It would have to be a player."

—Joe Trimble

October 4, 1964

Berra, in Bubbly Bath, Heaves Sigh, Taps Ford

by Norm Miller

Phil Linz, the unrepentant harmonicat, poured a bottle of champagne over Yogi Berra's head yesterday and got away with it. Linz laughed as the bubbly stuff streamed down the boss' face; Yogi went along with the gag and all the Yankees joined in, too.

A newsman asked for his opening World Series pitcher.

"Ford!" he hollered. "And probably Stottlemyre in the second game, no matter where it's played. All those National League parks are small and Whitey and Stottlemyre are sinkerball pitchers."

Did it matter whom the Yanks played?

"I don't care who wins in the National League as long as we're in," Berra replied. "I wouldn't want their race to end in a play-off, though. We want to start playing Wednesday. It wouldn't do us any good to wait the extra days."

Mantle confessed that he had given up on the Yankees' chances of winning "around the middle of the season."

"This has been the toughest race I've been in," said the Mick. "I didn't think we could make it for a while back there. We'd lost four straight to Chicago. I was out of the lineup and Whitey and some of the other pitchers were hurt. It just seemed that everything was going against us." ∎

CORKING GOOD SHOW, MEN. Yankees celebrate after clinching the franchise's 29th pennant by beating the Indians, 8-3, at the Stadium. The victors (l. to r.): Bobby Richardson, Tony Kubek, Pete Mikkelson (with Elston Howard backing him up), Phil Linz, and Yogi Berra. (News photo by Dan Farrell.)

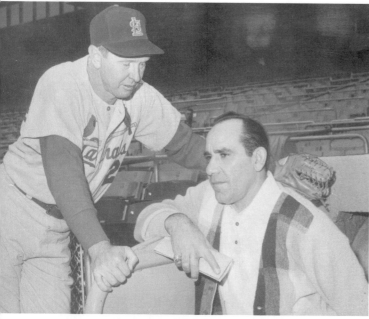

Two of the most popular figures in recent baseball history, Cardinal coach Red Schoendienst (l.) and Yankee manager Yogi Berra compare notes in the Stadium stands. They last faced each other as players in the 1957 and '58 Series. (News photo by Charles Hoff.)

Berra Welcomes Cards as WS Foes for Yanks

by Joe Trimble

October 5, 1964—Yogi Berra is going home, but he'll be cast as the villain— not the returning hero—when he leads the Yankees against the Cardinals in the World Series Wednesday. The kid who worshipped the Redbirds when he was growing up on "The Hill" is happy the Birds won the NL flag.

"It will be good to go home," he said yesterday after the Yankees closed out the season with a 13-inning, 2-1 loss to the Indians.

"I didn't care which of the clubs won over there, just as long as there was no play-off. We wanted to get started without a delay."

Berra named Whitey Ford as his first-game pitcher, and indicated Mel Stottlemyre would go in the second one, with Jim Bouton opening in New York next Saturday.

"Will it be a three-pitcher Series [three starters] or four?" he was asked.

"I don't know," he said. "Probably four. I'll have to see how it goes. Downing is the fourth one, but I'll also have him in the bullpen. He helped me that way when the relievers had those sore arms in August."

Visions of big Yankee bats dance in Yogi's head. Yogi is flanked by his sluggers, Mickey Mantle, Ellie Howard, and Roger Maris. (News photo by Dan Farrell.)

October 16, 1964

Cards Take It All as Yanks Fold, 7-5

4 Bad Throws Offset 3 Home Runs; Gibson Fans 9 in Final for Record

by Joe Trimble

The Yankees "threw" the World Series away today when they lapsed afield again and lost the seventh and deciding game to the Cardinals, 7-5. They didn't throw it in the gambling sense, of course, but four bad throws helped the new World Champions to four runs and made the difference.

The horrible heaves wiped out the effects of a three-run homer by Mickey Mantle, the Switcher's 18th Series swat and a record, as well as ninth-inning bombs by two less likely Bombers, Clete Boyer and Phil Linz.

So all the New York runs came on homers off big Bob Gibson, the St. Louis right-hander who fanned nine more today and set a Series record with 31 strikeouts. The win was the second in succession for the former Harlem Globetrotter, the outstanding pitcher in the Series.

Three of the terrible throws helped the Cardinals to three runs in the fourth inning and forced the removal of Mel Stottlemyre for a pinch hitter, depriving the Yankees of their fine rookie pitcher.

The Cards then jumped on Al Downing for three more in the fifth and a 6-0 lead. The crowd of 30,346 began the horn-tooting celebration a la New Year's Eve at that point and continued it to the end, although sobered slightly by the Bomber home runs.

"These were two pretty evenly matched teams," Berra observed after the game. "It seemed to me that every break they got they capitalized on; and every time we made an error, they scored."

Everyone on the Yankees had extreme praise for Cardinal pitcher Bob Gibson. "He's a hell of a pitcher," Howard said. "He doesn't give you anything to hit at."

"Gibson had pretty good stamina," Berra said, "especially after going 10 innings on Monday."

There was no champagne in the losers' dressing room, and the players spurned even the free beer.

They weren't happy losers. ∎

BERRA FINDS OUT ABOUT 1965 FROM DAN TODAY

by Jim McCulley and Dick Young

October 16, 1964—Yogi Berra has a noon date tomorrow to play golf with his Montclair buddies, but probably won't make it because he was notified today that Dan Topping wants to see him about a 1965 contract.

"I can't tell you where the meeting is going to be held," Yogi told newsmen, "except that it'll be in New York."

When Yogi signed his first contract to manage the Yankees, he was asked: "What do you think your main problem will be?"

"To see if I can manage," Yogi had answered.

"Well . . .," a reporter said today.

"I think I can do it," Yogi smiled.

YOGI KICKED OUT
KEANE RESIGNS

Stories on Page 30

(NEWS foto by Ed Molinari).
At Savoy Hilton Hotel, Yankee GM Ralph Houk announces Yogi Berra's removal as club's pilot. Houk said "move will be beneficial to all concerned."

Rival World Series managers Johnny Keane (left) and Yogi Berra embrace in victorious St. Louis dressing room Thursday afternoon after Cards had edged Yankees for world's championship. Now for later developments see the Fuke at right

What a Difference
A Day Makes

Cards' general manager Bob Howsam (left) and owner August Busch listen as Johnny Keane tells reporters "I'm looking for a job." Keane, in surprise move, quit a good one yesterday as skipper of the Cardinals. Busch said he "was shocked" when Keane refused to change his mind.

Stories on page 30

October 17, 1964

Series DP: Keane to Succeed Yogi

Yogi Ousted but Stays as Houk Aid

by Jim McCulley and Joe Trimble

In a weird rewrite of *A Tale of Two Cities*—New York and St. Louis—Yogi Berra yesterday was fired as Yankee manager, with resigned Cardinal pilot Johnny Keane ticketed to handle the Bronx Bombers next spring. General manager Ralph Houk stunned a press conference at the Savoy Plaza in making the Berra announcement but added that Yogi had signed a contract with the club as a "special field consultant" for the next two years.

THE NEWS learned of Keane's taking over the managerial assignment late last night, when an authoritative source said the decision was made as long ago as three weeks.

The morale of the Yanks was at a low point earlier in the season and when Houk traveled with the team he saw the breakdown firsthand.

THE NIGHT People were taking advantage of Yogi and the Day People resented the lack of discipline by Yogi. The hard feelings threatened to split the team wide open during the late stages of the pennant race but both factions, somehow, managed to pull together till the flag was clinched.

Berra was as stunned as anyone at his dismissal but the opposing factions on the club forced Houk's hand.

BERRA, WHO DID not attend the press conference, was reached at White Beeches CC, Haworth, N.J., where he had a golf date with friends. Berra said of his dismissal as manager: "I don't mind. I'll be spending a year at home. Where can you get a job like this? I don't have to sign in or punch a clock and the pay is good (about $25,000, which is 10G under what he was paid to manage and 20G under what he earned in his final year as a player).

"I called my wife the first thing," he said. "She said it was all right with her for me to do what I wanted to do.

"I SUPPOSE I'll be doing some scouting in the minors and majors. My contract is nonbinding and if another offer turns up I'm free to take it," Berra told a reporter.

Dressed for golf in a yellow shirt and brown trousers, Berra said: "I feel pretty good. Why shouldn't I? We won the pennant and it took seven games to beat us in the Series."

HOUK SAID THE fact the Yanks lost the Series to the Cards had nothing to do with Berra's sacking. "The decision was made before the World Series," Houk said.

Houk said the decision was made by Topping and himself; that nobody from the Columbia Broadcasting System, the new Yankee owners, was consulted about the change.

Insiders knew Berra's job as manager was in jeopardy in mid-August, when the club slipped $5\frac{1}{2}$ games back of the lead. The players talked about it pretty freely among themselves. But when the Yanks rallied to win the flag for their old buddy, Yogi's job seemed safe for at least another year. ■

Bad Guys and Good Guys Put Yogi in the Middle

by Joe Trimble

Yogi Berra wasn't fired by the Yankee brass. His own players, both the good boys and the playboys, pulled the rug out from under him. In what was one of the most bizarre byplays in baseball history, the Night Riders of the Yankees got out of control and the Day People so resented it they made it impossible for Ralph Houk to keep Berra as manager.

Bobby Richardson and Tony Kubek stated flatly that they would not return under Berra next season. Elston Howard, another veteran, had this opinion:

"The man can't control these guys," Howard said honestly.

Berra's Fate Sealed in August

Berra hoped all the fomentation would subside and the dirty linen would be dispensed with when the team rallied and won the pennant. But he didn't know that his fate had been decided back in mid-August, when the Bombers seemed to be falling completely out of the race.

Swimming-pool high-jinks at night in Hollywood, and vivid parties in Chicago and its suburbs, plus individual rule-breaking led to a *La Dolce Vita* clique on the one hand and a group of serious-minded athletes on the other. There was bound to be a clash when it looked as though the wild men had blown the pennant and the World Series loot, depriving the good guys of thousands of dollars apiece.

The "Harmonica Incident" was blown up out of proportion. It did pinpoint the defiance of Berra's authority. Phil Linz isn't a bad kid at all. In fact, he rates as a good one.

The full story behind the harmonica bit hasn't been told until you read this: It was in Chicago in August, when the Yanks blew four in a row to the White Sox.

Music-minded Trio Brought Harmonicas

On the afternoon of the final night game of that bad series, Wednesday, Aug. 19, roommates Richardson and Kubek bought a Billy Graham hymnbook. It had musical notes corresponding to the words. Let Richardson's words tell the story from there.

"Tony and I decided we'd like to sing the hymns and we wanted to have music. Harmonicas seemed right. So we started from the hotel to walk over to Marshall Field [department store] to buy them. Linz met us outside the hotel, had nothing to do, and we invited him along.

"We went up to the eighth floor, where they sold harmonicas, and Tony and I each bought one. We took the escalator to the seventh floor and Linz suddenly decided he'd like to have one, too. So he asked us to wait while he went back up to buy one."

Linz, of course, was imprudent enough to play the mouth organ in the bus en route to O'Hare Field after the Yanks had lost their fourth in a row the following afternoon. And he sassed Berra when Yogi told him to cut it out. Phil was fined $200 for his recital after the team arrived in Boston, where two more losses ran the reverse string to six before the boys began to fly right.

That's the kind of ball club this was: one set of guys playing hymns and another set playing at the Playboy Club.

Linz, a reserve infielder, was the only Yankee fined. And he had to be, because his defiance was public knowledge. Berra knew of the nightlife and drinking of the players who were so inclined, but he didn't do anything to stop it.

Previous Managers Had Same Problem

Of course, it didn't start in his one season as manager. It went on under Joe McCarthy, Bucky Harris, Casey Stengel, and Houk. But all four were strong enough to jack up the night owls and make them play ball when the chips were down. Indeed, the after-hours activity led to Harris' dismissal, when he lost control in the 1948 season.

Houk actually made up his mind that Berra could not handle the club when he saw things for himself on a road trip. It was in mid-August that he began to think about a successor.

"I spent many a sleepless night thinking it over," Houk confided recently. "But I felt it was the right decision for the good of the ball club."

Actually, the winning of the pennant embarrassed the front office, in the sense that it made the firing of the lovable Yogi more difficult. But once Dan Topping, who runs the store for CBS, and Houk made up their minds, there was no changing. Yogi was a dead duck, even if he had won the World Series from the man who succeeded him so shortly thereafter.

In sum, the players burned the candle at both ends and Yogi wound up being seared. ■

That's show business: Yank Berra muses over *The News'* story of the CBS purchase of the Yankees. (News photo by Charles Hoff.)

Managers Stengel and Berra before the Mayor's Trophy Game at Shea Stadium. (News photo by Godrey.)

October 30, 1964

Berra Gets Bid From Mets; Reply Expected in 10 Days

by Joe Trimble

Yogi Berra a Met? What could be more wonderful? The deposed Yankee manager yesterday received a definite offer from the Mets and will let them know in about 10 days if he will accept the offer—and a reunion with his old boss, Casey Stengel.

"I talked with Yogi on the phone," Met president George Weiss said. "He is going to Pinehurst [N.C.] on a golfing vacation and will think things over. I contacted him after a mutual friend said he would be interested.

"I WOULD LIKE to have a man like Berra, for his baseball knowledge and popularity. When I talked with him, he had not signed a contract with the Yankees."

Commissioner Ford Frick said Wednesday that Ralph Houk, Yankee GM, had assured him Yogi was free to go anywhere he liked—signed or not. ∎

Another former Yankee, Met President George Weiss, shows Yogi around the offices at Shea Stadium. Yogi, whom Casey called "my assistant manager" in the Yankee days, could possibly someday become Casey's successor to the headaches of managing the Mets. (News photo by John Duprey.)

November 18, 1964—HELLO, YOGI. IT'S SO NICE TO HAVE YOU . . . Met Yogi Berra looks over his new home field, Shea Stadium, after the Mets announced he had signed as coach—and later as a player—yesterday. The deposed Yank pilot received his $25,000 farewell present from the Yanks.

Player-Coach Yogi Shifts to Shea

by Dick Young

Yogi Berra yesterday took the Met job to coach and play a bit, and at the gala press conference at Shea for some 100 newsmen and fotogs, they set up a long-distance telephonic interview, involving the new coach and manager Casey Stengel in California, and what do you suppose happened? Stengel was cut off, not once, but three times. They finally gave up on the gimmick, and Berra, right away quick, felt like a Met.

Berra signed for two years, at $40,000 per year, and it is just a coaching contract right now, but that will be torn up in the spring and a player-coach contract signed. This is a gambit necessitated by the preciousness of roster space at present. The Mets have 40 players on the frozen roster, leaving them room to make one draft pick at the upcoming meetings. Were they to put Yogi on the roster immediately, they would forfeit their chance to draft.

Berra, who will be 40 in May, said he has no guarantee he will be groomed to succeed Stengel as manager of the

Mets, but admitted he hopes to learn much about managing from the Old Master—"if a chance to manage again comes along."

Berra's first chance to manage lasted one year. He took over the Yankees last season, when Ralph Houk moved up to general manager. Yogi won the pennant,

Yogi Berra signs autographs for Peace Corps Director Sargent Shriver, Father of the Year, at the Waldorf-Astoria. Bert Lahr, Stage Father, is a one-man audience. Yogi was named Sports Father of the Year by the National Fathers' Day Committee. Shriver, brother-in-law of the late President Kennedy, has four children, ranging in age from three months to ten years. (News photo by Charles Hoff.)

lost the World Series, and was canned a day later. Houk said at the time it was "for the good of all concerned."

Yesterday, as Berra submitted to a barrage of questions, he was asked if he had been told specifically why the Yankees fired him.

"Yes," he said.

"Why?"

Berra laughed. "No comment," he said.

It is generally believed the Yankee brass felt Berra had lost disciplinary control of the ball players, if he ever had it. When he took the job, he had been warned of the inherent weakness involved: trying to clamp down on players he had been a teammate of, a buddy of.

"Do you feel you took a scupping from the Yankees?" a newsman said during the Q&A period.

"No, I don't feel that way," Berra said. "I have no regrets. I was very happy with the Yankees."

YOGI'S YEAR

Yogi Berra was honored yesterday as Sports Father of the Year at the annual awards luncheon of the National Father's Day Committee at the Waldorf-Astoria. Yogi and his wife, Carmen, have three sons, Larry Jr., 14, Timmy, 12, and Dale, 7.

Berra is the seventh Yankee to win this award, starting with Babe Ruth in 1947. In between the honor was presented to Phil Rizzuto in '51; Mickey Mantle in '57; Bob Turley in '58; Ralph Houk in '60, and Tom Tresh last year.

In answer to questions about returning to action, Berra said: "I'll go to spring training, and get in shape, and see what happens. I'm not in bad shape. I caught batting practice every day with the Yankees in Florida last spring."

Berra didn't play during his managerial year. He did pinch-hit twice in exhibitions—once in an old-timers' game and again in the Yankee-Met clash for the Mayor's Trophy. Each time, Yogi hit into a DP, and it is his embarrassed boast that he made four outs in two at-bats.

As a player-coach with the Yankees the year before, Berra went to bat 147 times, hit .293, and cracked eight homers. If he can approximate that with the Mets, he would win the Rambler awarded annually to their best player.

Undoubtedly Berra will work the first-base line. Everybody seemed a bit coy about that yesterday, but obviously the Mets didn't hire Yogi to hide him in the dugout or the bullpen. He will be a showpiece. ∎

"You can't think and hit at the same time."

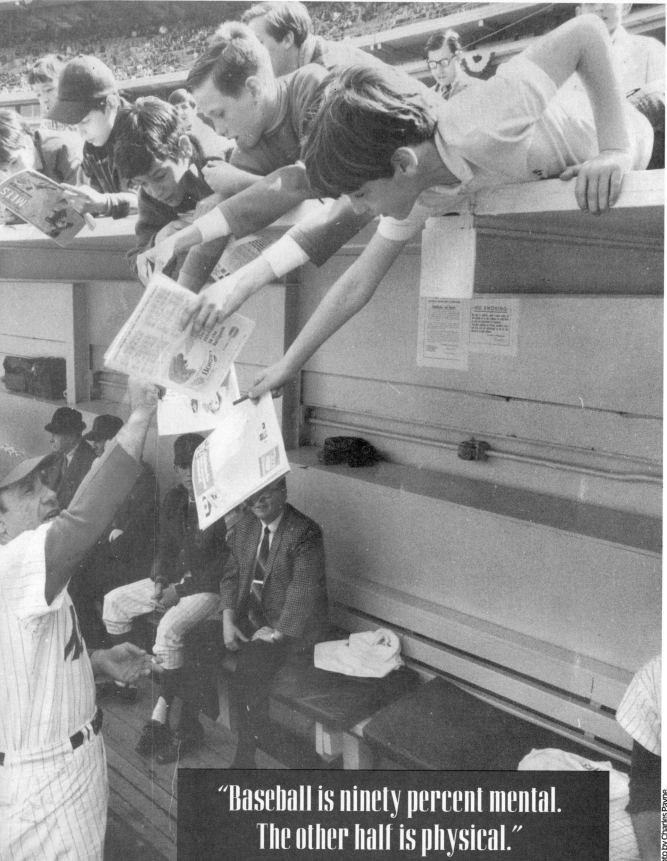

"Baseball is ninety percent mental.
The other half is physical."

12

1965-68: Not So Amazing

Mets Final Standings: 1965-68				
	W.	L.	PCT.	G.B.
1965	50	112	.309	47
1966	66	95	.410	$28^{1}/_{2}$
1967	61	101	.377	$40^{1}/_{2}$
1968	73	89	.451	24

After being fired as Yankee manager, Yogi became a coach for the inept but endearing New York Mets, rejoining former Yankee manager Casey Stengel. Founded in 1962, the Mets had a reputation for being hapless and hopeless, prompting Stengel's famous question: "Can't anybody here play this game?" Regardless, the team had garnered a supportive following despite their difficulties on the field.

The legendary Stengel, the first Mets manager, was forced to retire during the 1965 season because of a broken hip. He was replaced by Wes Westrum, who managed through 1967. Salty Parker also managed 11 games in 1967.

Gil Hodges, who had played for the Mets in the later stages of his career, returned to the club from the Washington Senators and took over the managerial reins in 1968. His team finished the season in a dismal ninth place, but brighter days were just around the corner. ∎

Yogi Berra, former Yankee, and Tommy Davis, former Dodger, both now wearing Mets uniforms, flank former Dodger great Roy Campanella.

Yogi Retires as Player

by Dick Young

Yogi Berra, a magic name in baseball, last night retired as an active player after a two-week comeback that led only to the conclusion that he no longer has it.

The decision was made minutes before his 40th birthday, today. He and the other Met coaches, and Casey Stengel, and the people from the front office conferred immediately after last night's game to discuss getting down to the 25-player limit at the stroke of midnight.

Yogi, even here, had one night of glory. A week ago, he caught Al Jackson against the Phils. He got his only two hits. He scored the winning run. Yogi knew it was an illusion. "It's hard for me to see the ball," he said later.

Today, Yogi is 40, and a coach. One day, he will be in the Hall of Fame. ∎

Met coach Yogi Berra admires the strawberry-bedecked 40th birthday cake presented to him at Shea Stadium by members of the official Met team and office personnel. (News photo by Charles Hoff.)

Brigadier General Andrew S. Miller presents the Salvation Army Red Shield Award of Merit to Mets coach Yogi Berra, who accepts it on behalf of the N.Y. Mets. (News photo Dan Farrell.)

Yogi Berra, new sales promotion coordinator for a Seventh Ave. textile firm, shows wares to a potential customer, his wife, Carmen. (News photo by Judd Mehlman.)

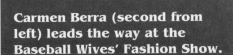

Carmen Berra (second from left) leads the way at the Baseball Wives' Fashion Show.

METS MAKE A HIT. Met outfielder Ron Swoboda (l.) autographs a baseball for Richard Muriel, in Bellevue Hospital. Coach Yogi Berra is on deck with a bat for the youngster. Met players visited Bellevue with presents for the kids. (News photo by Hal Mathewson.)

PAYING HOMAGE TO A GRAND OLD MAN. Casey lets go with a few words in his own inimitable style to the delight of former Yankee greats, standing (l. to r.): Allie Reynolds, Tommy Byrne, Joe DiMaggio, Vic Raschi, Tom Henrich and Bill Dickey. Flanking Casey are Phil Rizzuto (l.) and Yogi Berra.

Yogi Berra samples cake for Casey Stengel's 75th birthday celebration at Shea Stadium. (News photo by Charles Hoff.)

The newest Met, Chuck Hiller (l.), amazes Casey Stengel by signing the boss' cast, while Yogi Berra looks on in the dugout at Stea Stadium. (News photo by Charles Hoff.)

Yogi Berra and Rocky Graziano. (News photo by David McLane.)

COLORFUL GUYS. Mets manager Casey Stengel (left) and coach Yogi Berra beam approval of the page-one color photo of themselves in *The News*. (News photo by Paul DeMaria.)

THE GIANTS OF THE CITY'S BASEBALL SCENE. Met coach Yogi Berra scratches his head, possibly in wonder at how Giant Willie Mays can stay young so long. The two longtime heroes of New York baseball buffs met at Shea before the season-opening clash between the two teams.

CHARACTERS GETTIN' READY FOR A SHOW. *News* cartoonist Bill Gallo (l.), who's looking more like Basement Bertha every day, gets together with Joe Garagiola, Yogi Berra, and *News* scribe Joe Trimble to study the script for the Baseball Writers dinner and show at the Americana Hotel. With a cast like this, who needs actors? (News photo by Charlie Payne.)

BRINGING THE GOOD NEWS. Edward Chrzastet, a 12-year-old Met fan, was one of the early arrivals at Shea Stadium, and the first one he wanted to see was Yogi Berra, who obliged by autographing a copy of the color photo which appeared on page one of *The News*. (News photo by Dan Farrell.)

★★★★ FiNAL

DAILY NEWS

NEW YORK'S PICTURE NEWSPAPER ®

8¢

10¢ OUTSIDE L.I. AND SUBURBS

Vol. 51. No. 98   Copr. 1969 News Syndicate Co. Inc.   New York, N.Y. 10017, Friday, October 17, 1969*   WEATHER: Partly cloudy, breezy, cool.

WORLD CHAMPS!

"We have deep depth."

13

1969: Amazing Champions

I n a mere seven seasons, the New York Mets had acquired a national reputation. Unfortunately for the players and coaches, their fame stemmed not from their success in building a dynasty but from their well-documented difficulties on the field. But in a city still mourning the desertion of the Dodgers and the Giants after the 1957 season, the Mets secured a large following, and their fans loved them in spite of themselves.

On October 16, 1969, the Amazing Mets stunned the baseball world and brought joy back to New York City. In a miraculous reversal of fortune, they rewarded their faithful fans by catapulting from a dismal ninth-place finish in 1968 to triumph as the unexpected champions of the National League. Continuing their miraculous turnaround, the Mets next defeated the Baltimore Orioles four games to one in the 1969 World Series, inspiring underdogs everywhere and becoming baseball's newest World Champions. ■

The best banner of 'em all flies over the heads of the fans who believe in miracles. They also believed in the Mets. (News photo by Ed Clarity.)

October 17, 1969

Hallelujah! Mets Top World!

4th in Row Leaves Birds for Dead, 5-3

by Phil Pepe

No more worlds to conquer. No more miracles to perform. No more disbelievers to convince. The Mets are World Champions.

The eight-year-old, onetime ragamuffin, perennial doormat, not-to-be-believed Mets are the baseball champions of all the world, and all the superlatives used when they won the National League pennant can be trotted out again and they still will not be sufficient to describe the joy and the satisfaction of this World Championship.

"What next?" said one sign the moment the Mets completed yesterday's 5-3 victory and became the World Champions, and there was no answer, really, for the question.

"There are no words" said another sign and, indeed, it is difficult to put into words the extraordinary, incredible events of the last few hours, the last few days, the last few weeks, the last few months.

The Mets won it convincingly, four games to one over the American League Orioles, a so-called super team which had won 109 of 162 games in its league, had won its division title by 19 games and had rolled through its play-off, as the Mets had, in a three-game sweep.

And the Mets won yesterday's clincher in typical Met fashion,

refusing to quit when they fell behind, 3-0, and coming on to win with so many heroes that when it came time to name a series MVP there was support for five Mets.

When Cleon Jones gathered in Davey Johnson's drive at the warning track in left, it was the heart-pounding climax not of nine exciting innings, not of a remarkable year, it was the climax of eight frustration-filled years that began with Casey Stengel and ended with Gil Hodges. It was the fulfillment of a dream that began when the Dodgers and Giants moved out of New York in 1957 and now, a dozen years later, the Mets have won one more World Championship than the San Francisco Giants.

Winning pitcher Jerry Koosman jumps on his batterymate, Jerry Grote, after Cleon Jones caught Davey Johnson's fly ball for the final out of the year. Donn Clendenon (22), who put the Mets back in the game with his homer in the sixth inning, rushes in to join the celebration. (News photo Paul DeMaria.)

It was a victory for the 57,397 fans in Shea yesterday and the millions more who would have been there if they could. It was a victory for all the underdogs in all the sports through all the years that athletics have been a vital part of this country.

And it was a victory that, Ron Swoboda said as only Ron Swoboda can say, "will give heart to every loser in America."

In the end, they made Donn Clendenon the Most Valuable Player and it was a fitting choice because Donn Clendenon, like the Mets, represents a storybook rags-to-riches fable. When this season started, Donn Clendenon was working for an Atlanta pen company. Today, he is a World Series hero and there is no hero like a World Series hero.

They gave the MVP award to Donn Clendenon and it was fitting, but it would have been just as fitting—and just as deserved—if they had given it to Jerry Koosman, who was discovered pitching army ball and yesterday pitched the World Series clincher; or to Tommie Agee, who was a flop in 1968 and a team leader in 1969; or to Al Weis, who was cast off by the White Sox two years ago and hit the game-tying home run yesterday; or to Ron Swoboda, who lived through five years of frustration as a Met and yesterday knocked in the wining run with a double.

The Mets won it the way they wanted to win it and they won it where they wanted to win it—in Shea Stadium. They did not want to return to Baltimore. They had seen Baltimore; there was no need to see it again.

But it seemed as if the return trip to Baltimore would be necessary when the Orioles' bats, silent throughout the last three games, finally exploded against Koosman in the third to give the Birds a 3-0 lead.

Oriole pitcher Dave McNally carried his 3-0 lead into the sixth and then the miracle worker awoke from his afternoon slumber. Cleon Jones was hit in the right foot by a pitch. That's what Cleon Jones said. That's what on-deck hitter Donn Clendenon said. And that's what Gil Hodges said. Plate ump Lou DiMuro said no, but Hodges produced the ball and showed DiMuro the mark right next to Warren Giles' signature and DiMuro was convinced. He waved Cleon to first.

Clendenon followed Jones at bat. Naturally, he hit a 2-2 pitch into the second deck in left for his third Series home run. The score was now 3-2. The miracle worker was doing his stuff.

Al Weis led off the Mets' seventh. Al Weis came to bat and the sign man behind third base held up a sign that said: "Believe in Miracles?" Then he held up another sign: "We Believe." And Al Weis, who makes 165 on the scale when he has lead weights in each pocket, and who can't hit a ball that far, hit one into the left-field bleachers, 375 feet away, to tie it, 3-3.

Now the outcome was inevitable to everyone in Shea. Forget it, Birds. Fly back to your nests. This is not the Year of the Bird; it is the Year of the Met, whatever that is. It is the year of New York over Baltimore—the Jets over the Colts, the Knicks over the Bullets, the Mets over the Orioles.

Jerry Koosman was all right now. He retired the Orioles in order in the eighth—he had allowed just one single since the third—and the Mets were coming to bat in the last of the eighth and throughout the stands there was that certain feeling.

After the Mets scored twice in their half of the eighth, to take a 5-3 lead, the ninth inning began with the kids starting to assemble in the runways, ready to spring into action with the third out, ready to dash onto the field, ready to make their onslaught of the turf.

Frank Robinson opened the Orioles' ninth with a walk, but huge, awesome, frightening Boog Powell tapped to second and Robby was forced. Brooks Robinson flied deep to right and the Orioles were down to their last out and the kids were ready to make their charge.

Davey Johnson's final drive was hit good, deep to left, and for a split second, hearts stopped. But the mystical force that has worked all year for the Mets held the ball up and made it come down softly in Cleon's glove.

Now bedlam. All the Mets were out on the field. Jerry Grote was climbing on Jerry Koosman. They were embracing. Ron Swoboda did a Ron Santo heel click as he neared the Mets' dugout. And the kids were all over the place grabbing their souvenirs—caps, bases, flags, clumps of grass, anything they could get their hands on and move.

For the third time in three weeks, champagne flowed in the Mets' clubhouse. For the third time in three weeks, players and fans were going through an emotion-draining celebration. For the third time in three weeks, Shea Stadium was left for rubble.

Now the Mets could turn the field over to the Jets. They wouldn't be needing it anymore. They had worked their miracles for this year. ■

■ KEEPIN' UP ■

Cleon Jones, 27, was told after yesterday's game that another Jones had also helped win a World Series by being hit on the foot with a "shoeshine ball."

The reference was to the Braves' Nippy Jones, who was hit on the shoe in the 1957 WS against the Yanks by Tommy Byrne in the 10th inning of the fourth game. The Braves won the game, 6-5, and went on to win the Series.

Cleon said: "Well, you have to keep up with the Joneses."

'Worse Than Clincher'

October 17, 1969—There was a madhouse on the field, as well in the clubhouse, after the Mets finished their unreal year yesterday at Shea. "Wait till Weeb Ewbank sees this," said one of the many special policemen who were unable to keep thousands of people of all ages from tearing the field apart. The Jets are due to play there next Monday night and, of course, will.

"Much worse than it was after we clinched the pennant," conceded Johnny McCarthy, whose overworked ground crew immediately began to repair the damage. "We'll do our best to get it ready, but we've lost an awful lot of turf."

About twice the amount of sod that was lifted after the clincher was cut up and carted away yesterday, rolled in blankets and carried in boxes and paper bags brought for the purpose.

More than 50 of the unanchored special box seats were captured but the specials were able to recapture almost all of them. Another favorite souvenir was the center-field fence. Several large hunks of it were ripped off and carried away.

A blizzard of ticker tape, confetti, and torn telephone books cascades on lower Broadway as a motorcade carrying the team to City Hall starts up the Canyon of Heroes. (News photo by Jack Smith.)

October 16, 1969

Mets Drive Birds Cuckoo in 10, 2-1

Gaspar Scored Winner on Richert Wild Throw

by Phil Pepe

All the skeptics and cynics who wondered how a team like the Mets could win the National League pennant had only to show up at Shea Stadium yesterday to get their answer.

In winning a 2-1, 10-inning thriller from the Orioles in Game No. 4 of the World Series, the Mets shot the works and pulled out all of their particular talents—tough pitching and spectacular glovework on defense. The Orioles helped the Mets' offense with a misjudged fly-ball double and a bad throw. The victory gives the Mets a 3-1 edge in games and leaves them one short of being crowned World Champions in their eighth year of existence and with three chances to get it. Jerry Koosman, who beat the Birds in game two, gets a chance to wrap it up today against Dave McNally.

Unable to win in the regulation nine, the Mets used their best shots to win it in the frenetic 10th on a bunt by pinch hitter J.C. Martin. When reliever Pete Richert fielded Martin's sac bunt and threw hurriedly to first, the ball struck Martin in the left wrist and bounded toward second as the winning run crossed the plate.

In answer to the question, "Who the hell is Rod Gaspar?" the Orioles will remember him as the Met who carried the winning run home.

Gaspar was on base as a runner for Jerry Grote, who led off the 10th with a routine fly to short left. Don Buford, the Orioles' left fielder, misjudged the ball momentarily and started back to the fence. When he realized the ball was not hit that far and changed direction, it was too late, and it plopped in short left out of reach of Buford, centerfielder Paul Blair, and shortstop Mark Belanger.

Gaspar's legs replaced Grote's legs at second and Oriole coach Billy Hunter ordered Al Weis intention-

A PERFECT ENDING FOR A PERFECT DAY. J.C. Martin, author of the bunt that went awry, gets an affectionate reception from Yogi (No. 8) and his teammates as he comes off the field. (News photo by Mel Finkelstein.)

ally walked to set up the force. Hunter was calling the shots because manager Earl Weaver was banished by plate ump Shag Crawford for protesting a called strike to Mark Belanger in the third.

Now the Mets had runners on first and second with none out and Gil Hodges sent Martin to bunt for starting pitcher Tom Seaver against righty Dick Hall. Now it was Hunter's turn. Out came Hall, in came lefty Richert to pitch to lefty Martin.

J.C. did his job. His bunt was a beauty, equidistant between Richert coming in and catcher Elrod Hendricks going out. For a split second there was indecision, but Richert ran Hendricks off the ball and made the play himself. He had to hurry to get Martin and his throw was low and on the infield side of first base. Ball and runner came together a stride in front of the bag and Martin felt the ball bounce off his left wrist, then he saw it trickle toward second base.

Third-base coach Eddie Yost saw it, too, and so did Rod Gaspar, and so did the Mets bench, and so did the 57,367 fans, and everybody was yelling and screaming and urging Gaspar to score. He didn't need any urging and he crossed the plate standing up, and then the entire Met bench was out to greet him and to pound his back and hug him in the ritual of victory. ■

Shag Still Has Last Word, J.C. Didn't Step Out of Line

by Dana Mozley

October 17, 1969—Pictures to the contrary, the final, hectic play of the Amazin' Mets' fourth-game victory Wednesday has been ruled perfectly legal. Plate umpire Shag Crawford, who had the responsibility of calling any interference play down the first-base line, declared it so and Commissioner Bowie Kuhn backed him up.

Pictures showed that, after laying down his perfect bunt, J.C. Martin was running to first inside the baseline. Pitcher Pete Richert's throw hit him on the left wrist and ricocheted toward second base, runner Rod Gaspar coming all the way from second to score the winner.

As the rule is written, Martin could have been charged with interference, called out, and Gaspar returned to second base.

Offered Crawford in rebuttal yesterday: "As I saw it, Martin had one foot [apparently the right one] on the line when struck by the ball. The picture was taken prior to the ball making contact."

Said Kuhn: "The umpire gave me his version of the play and I accepted that. It's a judgment call, like any close play at first base. It can be argued but not protested. If this were not so, we'd be playing all games over."

Said Martin, whose bruised and still sore wrist was wrapped in a bandage: "I ran straight down the line until Johnson [covering first] got in my collision line. To keep from running into him, I had to cut a little to the inside."

Tom Seaver (l.) and Jerry Koosman are mobbed. (News photo by Carmine Donofrio.)

While Yvonne Harrelson chats with Jerry Grote (l.) Cecelia Swoboda, Dianne DiLauor (hidden), and Sharon Grote talk with Mrs. Babe Ruth at the Gracie Mansion garden party after the 1969 World Series. (News photo by Gene Kappock.)

The Mets' first-base coach, Yogi Berra, is mobbed as he arrives at the Alfred E. Smith playground to join the neighborhood kids. (News photo by Dan Cronin.)

M—arvelous
E—xciting
T—oo Much; &
S—till Champs
Baseball commissioner Bowie Kuhn is on the field for a firsthand look at Mayor Lindsay's arm as the Mayor tosses out the first ball of the 1970 season at Shea. The opening-day cermonies included the raising of the Mets' 1969 World Championship banner. (News photo by Jim Garrett.)

"Baseball is the champ of them all. Like somebody said, the pay is good and the hours are short."

14

1971-72: Cooperstown Calling

In 1971, Yogi was a freshman candidate on the Hall of Fame ballot. Although he was the leading candidate, with 242 votes, he failed to win induction. As a result, the Baseball Writers' Association of America failed to elect a candidate for the first time in over 10 years. Election to the Hall of Fame requires 75 percent of the vote, and Yogi was 28 votes short. Despite disappointment, Yogi managed to put the matter in perspective, reminding himself that Joe DiMaggio also fell short in his first year of eligibility (1954).

In 1972, the baseball writers made up for the previous year, electing three candidates to baseball's Hall of Fame. Sandy Koufax received 344 votes, becoming only the fifth candidate to be elected in his first year of eligibility. Yogi received 339 votes, 42 more than the required 297. Early Wynn who was named on 301 ballots was also elected.

Yogi took a short break from his duties as a Mets coach to make the trip to Cooperstown for the induction ceremony on August 7, 1972. The induction of Koufax, Yogi, and Wynn brought the number of players in the Baseball Hall of Fame to 108. ■

Although the Baseball Writers' Association failed to elect anyone to the Hall of Fame in 1971, the Veteran's Committee saw fit to induct Rube Marquard (l.), and the Negro Leagues' Committee enshrined Satchel Paige (r.). (News photo by Dan Farrell.)

January 22, 1971

Berra Falls 28 Short of Hall of Fame

75% Rule Also Bars Wynn, Kiner

by Red Foley

The road to Cooperstown turned into a dead-end street for Yogi Berra yesterday. The onetime Yankee star was temporarily detoured from that path of glory when the Baseball Writers' Association annual poll failed to elect a candidate to the Hall of Fame.

Berra, with 242 votes, was 28 short of the required 75% needed for election. Early Wynn (240) and Ralph Kiner (212) trailed Yogi in the BBWAA's first negative result in more than a decade. Both Berra and Kiner are connected with the Mets; Yogi as a coach and Ralph as a member of the broadcasting team.

"Sure I'm disappointed," Berra said, "but then DiMag didn't make it his first year, either." The 45-year-old Met coach, a freshman candidate, was referring to the 1954 poll, in which Joe DiMaggio failed to achieve the needed three-fourths. The Yankee Clipper made it the following year.

Bob Feller, Ted Williams, Stan Musial, and Jackie Robinson were the only candidates ever to attain election in their first year of eligibility.

Berra, contacted at his Haworth [N.J.] golf club, expressed concern for the feelings of his three sons—Larry Jr., Dale, and Timmy. "They were all excited about this and it's going to be tough on them. But there's always next year for me."

Then, as in most of Yogi's conversations, his sense of humor took over. "Yeah," he added, "it's been a tough day all around. I don't get into the Hall of Fame this morning and this afternoon I'm over here [White Beeches CC] losing at gin rummy." ∎

Hall of Fame Vote

Yogi Berra (242); Early Wynn (240); Ralph Kiner (212); Gil Hodges (180); Enos Slaughter (165); Johnny Mize (157); Pee Wee Reese (127); Marty Marion (123); Red Schoendienst (123); Allie Reynolds (110); George Kell (105); John VanderMeer (98); Hal Newhouser (94); Phil Rizzuto (92); Bob Lemon (90); Duke Snider (89); Phil Cavaretta (83); Bobby Doerr (78); Al Dark (54); Nellie Fox (39); Bob Newsom (17); Dom DiMaggio (15); Charlie Keller (14); Mickey Vernon (12); John Sain (11); Harvey Haddix (10); Richie Asburn (10); Ted Kluszewski (9); Don Newcombe (8); Harry Brecheen (7), Walker Cooper (7); Wally Moses (7); Billy Pierce (7); Carl Furillo (5); Bobby Shantz (5); Bobby Thomson (4); Roy Sievers (4); Gil McDougald (4); Ed Lopat (4); Carl Erskine (3); Dutch Leonard (3); Preacher Rea (3); Vic Wertz (2); Vic Power (2); Vic Raschi (2); Wally Moon (2); Jackie Jensen (2); Bill Bruton (1); Frank Lary (0); Don Mossi (0).

January 20, 1972

Sandy, Yogi, and Wynn Run 1-2-3

by Joe Trimble

Like Ado Annie, the hostess in *Oklahoma*, the baseball writers couldn't say no to three of the game's former greats, enshrining Sandy Koufax, Yogi Berra, and Early Wynn in the Hall of Fame. Nobody made it last year.

Koufax made it in his first year of eligibility, being named on 344 of the 396 ballots. Yogi, former Yankee catcher and now Met coach, had 339, and Wynn, Washington, Cleveland, and Chicago pitcher, just barely made it with 301. The minimum for election was 297 votes, or 75% of those cast.

Koufax became only the fifth man to be elected first time around. The others were Ted Williams, Bob Feller, Jackie Robinson, and Stan Musial.

Berra, asked to identify the pitcher who gave him the most trouble, answered quickly: "Alex Kellner, the left-handed pitcher with the Athletics."

Berra said he wasn't disappointed when he wasn't named when he first became eligible last year. "It is great to make it, whether it takes one, two, three, or four years. It doesn't matter. Every ball player hopes to make it. This is the greatest honor of my life," he said.

Yogi revealed a surprise when he said that he had never batted against Koufax except in spring training.

"The year the Dodgers beat us four straight in the World Series [1963], I was the on-deck hitter when he got the final out in the fourth game."

Koufax was asked how he pitched to Berra the few times he did in exhibitions. He laughed again. "Very

Yogi Berra, who has never faced Sandy Koufax at the plate except in spring training, joins Sandy at the Americana yesterday. The Met coach and broadcaster had just learned that they, like Early Wynn, are rookies in the Hall of Fame. The threesome swells the ranks of baseball's pantheon to 108 and will be joining other greats on the Cooperstown wall August 7, when there will be a Yankee-Dodger game for old times' sake.

carefully," he answered. "Yogi didn't want you to throw strikes!"

Berra, best bad-ball hitter of his era, explained why. "People tried to make me wait for good pitches, particularly Casey [Stengel] but I told him the bad ones looked good to me when the ball was coming to the plate."

Of his 385 lifetime homers, Berra estimates that

only 20 or so came when he was not the catcher in the game.

The trio will be formally inducted in the Cooperstown shrine on Aug. 7. It is a happy coincidence that the Dodgers and Yanks meet in the exhibition game that day.

The addition of the three makes 108 players in the Hall of Fame. ∎

Daily News, **January 20, 1972**

Yogi's Hall of Fame Stats

Regular Season

Year	G	AB	H	HR	RBI	Avg.
1946	7	22	8	2	4	.364
1947	83	293	82	11	54	.280
1948	125	469	143	14	98	.305
1949	116	415	115	20	91	.277
1950	151	597	192	28	124	.322
1951	141	547	161	27	88	.294
1952	142	534	146	30	98	.273
1953	137	503	149	27	108	.296
1954	151	584	179	22	125	.307
1955	147	541	147	27	108	.272
1956	140	521	155	30	105	.298
1957	134	482	121	24	82	.251
1958	122	433	115	22	90	.266
1959	131	472	134	19	69	.284
1960	120	359	99	15	62	.276
1961	119	395	107	22	61	.271
1962	86	232	52	10	35	.224
1963	64	147	43	8	28	.293
1965	4	9	2	0	0	.222
Totals	2120	7555	2150	358	1430	.285

World Series

Year	G	AB	H	HR	RBI	Avg.
1947	6	19	3	1	2	.158
1949	4	16	1	0	1	.063
1950	4	15	3	1	2	.200
1951	6	23	6	0	0	.261
1952	7	28	6	2	3	.214
1953	6	21	9	1	4	.429
1955	7	24	10	1	2	.417
1956	7	25	9	3	10	.360
1957	7	25	8	1	2	.320
1958	7	27	6	0	2	.222
1960	7	22	7	1	8	.318
1961	4	11	3	1	3	.273
1962	2	2	0	0	0	.000
1963	1	1	0	0	0	.000
Totals	75	259	71	12	39	.274

All-Star Games

Year	G	AB	H	HR	RBI	Avg.
1948	1	0	0	0	0	.000
1949	1	3	0	0	0	.000
1950	1	2	0	0	0	.000
1951	1	4	1	0	0	.250
1952	1	2	0	0	0	.000
1953	1	4	0	0	0	.000
1954	1	4	2	0	0	.500
1955	1	6	1	0	0	.167
1956	1	2	2	0	0	1.000
1957	1	3	1	0	1	.333
1958	1	2	0	0	0	.000
1959	2	3	1	1	2	.333
1960	2	4	0	0	0	.000
1961	2	1	0	0	0	.000
1962	1	1	0	0	0	.000
Totals	18	41	8	1	3	.195

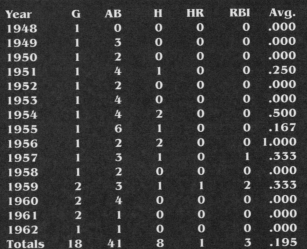

★★★★
FINAL

DAILY NEWS

NEW YORK'S PICTURE NEWSPAPER ©

10¢

Vol. 53. No. 242   Copr. 1972 New York News Inc.   New York, N.Y. 10017, Monday, April 3, 1972•   WEATHER: Sunny, breezy and cool.

GIL HODGES DIES OF HEART ATTACK

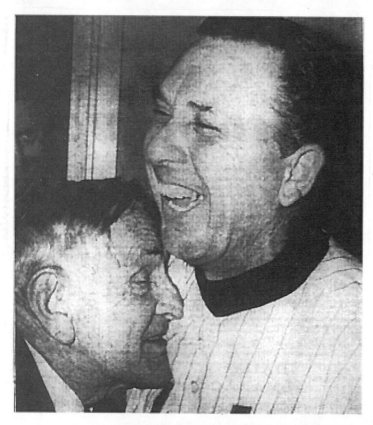

Mets' Boss Stricken After Round Of Golf

Mets' manager Gil Hodges, who died yesterday of a heart attack in West Palm Beach, Fla., after a round of golf, was hugged by original Mets' skipper Casey Stengel after the Cinderella Team won World Series in 1969. Hodges, who starred with the old Brooklyn Dodgers, would have been 48 tomorrow. Gil had suffered a mild heart attack during a Mets' game in Atlanta on Sept. 24, 1968. He returned the following year to lead the Mets to championship.

Stories on pages 3 and 67; other pictures on back page

"If you come to a fork in the road, take it."

15

1972: Taking Over in Tragedy

Yogi began 1972 prepared to serve another season as a coach for the Mets, but in April his life took an unexpected turn. Just days before the season was to start, Mets manager Gil Hodges suffered a heart attack and died in West Palm Beach, Florida, two days shy of his 48th birthday.

On April 6, the Mets chairman of the board, M. Donald Grant, announced that Yogi had been chosen as the new manager. Yogi signed a two-year contract and prepared to step into the role left vacant by Hodges' tragic death. In May, the Mets completed a deal that returned 41-year-old Willie Mays to New York City. Mays considered the deal a return to "Paradise," and assured the press that he could help the ball club.

Despite its sober beginning, the season was not without its happier moments. On July 26, at the 26th Oldtimers' Day at Yankee Stadium, the Yankees retired uniform number 8, worn by both

Yogi and Bill Dickey, the man who "learned" Yogi all his experiences. Though the Mets were playing in San Francisco, Larry Berra Jr. attended the ceremony and accepted the jersey on his father's behalf. ∎

Met chairman of the board, M. Don Grant, presents the new Met manager, Yogi Berra, in a somber announcement shortly after the death of Gil Hodges. (News photo by Nick Sorrentino.)

April 3, 1972

Mets' Hodges Dies in Florida of Heart Attack

by Red Foley

West Palm Beach, Fla.—Mets manager Gil Hodges suffered a fatal heart attack yesterday after a long afternoon of golf at Palm Beach Lakes Golf Club.

Hodges, who would have been 48 on Tuesday, was walking from the golf club back to the nearby Ramada Inn motel, where the Mets are quartered, when he collapsed at about 5:10 p.m.

He was taken by ambulance to Good Samaritan Hospital and admitted to the emergency room at 5:25, where he was treated by Dr. James Smith and cardiologist Dr. William Donovan.

Donovan said that an electrocardiogram showed "complete heart arrest," and Hodges was pronounced dead at 5:45.

The Met manager played 27 holes of golf with three Met coaches, Joe Rigatano, Rube Walker, and Eddie Yost, who were with him when he collapsed.

Hodges had suffered a mild heart attack during a Mets game in Atlanta on September 24, 1968, and spent several months recuperating before returning to guide the team to a startling and dramatic World Championship the following season.

Hodges' death left the Met official family in a state of shock. "I never saw him looking as well as he had this spring," said general manager, Bob Scheffing.

The rest of the Mets remaining here after the sport's first player strike began yesterday were similarly affected.

"Even if there weren't any strike, opening day wouldn't mean anything now," said shortstop Bud Harrelson, one of the players still here.

Mrs. Hodges had left West Palm Beach to return to her Brooklyn home on Friday. Gil Jr., who was in training at St. Petersburg, was on his way home last night.

Hodges' body is expected to arrive at LaGuardia Airport early tomorrow afternoon and will lie at the Andrew Torregrossa & Sons funeral home, 2265 Flatbush Ave., Brooklyn. Funeral arrangements were not complete late last night, but burial will be on Thursday in Brooklyn.

Hodges, a native of Princeton, Indiana, where he was born on April 4, 1924, married the former Joan Lombardi of Brooklyn in 1948, while he was starring for the Dodgers, and the family has made its home in Flatbush most of the time since. Besides his wife, Hodges is survived by a son, Gil Jr., 22, a minor league player in the Met organization, and three daughters, Irene, 21; Cynthia, 16; and Barbara, 11. ■

Yogi Berra and wife, Carmen, are among the mourners.

April 7, 1972

Berra Signs 2-Year Pact as Mets' Manager

by Joe Trimble

Yogi Berra yesterday became the fourth manager in Mets history. Berra agreed to a two-year contract Monday, but its announcement was withheld until four hours after the funeral of Gil Hodges, out of respect to the beloved manager, who died Easter Sunday in West Palm Beach.

As forecast by Dick Young in Wednesday's editions of *The News*, Yogi, "the only undefeated manager in baseball history," takes over a team he feels is on a par with the 1964 Yankees, whom he led to a pennant—the last one by the Bombers.

Berra was fired by then-owner Dan Topping after the loss to the Cardinals in the seven-game World Series. In one of baseball's weirdest twists, Johnny Keane, winning Series manager, quit St. Louis and became Berra's successor in '65.

Keane lacked support with the Yankee players and was replaced on May 7, 1966, by Ralph Houk, who stepped back down to field level from the general manager's chair. Houk had succeeded Casey Stengel as manager in 1961 and moved upstairs when Yogi took over in '64.

It was inevitable that Berra would be asked to compare the '64 Yanks with the '72 Mets. "I think this team has a better pitching staff. Not as much power as the Yanks did, but we will make more runs with the four hitters like Agee, Fregosi, Jonesy [Cleon Jones], and Staub coming up in a row."

Rusty Staub, of course, is the long-ball hitter obtained from Montreal in the deal announced yesterday.

"Nobody is going to be able to pitch around guys who can hit like them. I figure I'll bat Staub fourth against right-handers and fifth against left-handers.

"Naturally, I'm honored that I was chosen for the job by Mrs. Payson and Mr. Grant, but, of course, not at the way the job became open. We left a great man today and I only hope I can fill his shoes. Gil brought this club along perfectly in spring training and I think we have a winner."

Yogi was in Miami visiting with friends Sunday when Met board chairman Don Grant called him from his winter home in Hobe Sound, about 40 miles north of Palm Beach. He asked Berra to drive up to see him after offering him the job as manager. Yogi talked it over with his wife, Carmen, Sunday night and she advised: "Go ahead and take it."

Yogi claims he has no lasting feeling against the Yankees for being bounced after winning the pennant in his only year as manager. Carmen, however, has never forgiven the Bronx club.

Berra became a Met coach in 1965 and has worked under all three managers the Mets have had in their first 10 seasons—Casey Stengel, Wes Westrum, and Hodges.

Berra will be 47 on May 12. About two months later, he will be inducted into the Hall of Fame at Cooperstown along with Sandy Koufax and Early Wynn.

Yogi holds the record for most World Series games played (75) and most Series (14). The Yanks won 10 of those. He shares the one-season AL record of home runs by a catcher (30) with Gus Trinados. In 18 seasons he had a lifetime BA of .285 with 358 homers and 1,430 RBIs.

In his winning season as Yankee manager, the club seemed to be out of the race with three weeks of play left in September but then won the pennant with a remarkable stretch drive.

Berra said that he had never been promised a job as manager at any time during his career with the Mets, but added, " Naturally, I thought about it when that happened to Gil." ∎

New pilots Yogi Berra and Bill Virdon discuss their teams' chances before the start of the Mets-Pirates opener at Shea. (News photo by Frank Hurley.)

May 12, 1972

Mets Deal Brings Willie 'Back to Paradise'

by Red Foley

Willie Mays, saying it was like "coming back to Paradise," finally returned to New York yesterday. In a deal in which he got the divorce and Giants owner Horace Stoneham the alimony, the 41-year-old onetime superstar became a Met for what a beaming M. Donald Grant hopes "will be the rest of Willie's life."

Mays, expected to debut in a Met uniform against the Giants at Shea on Sunday, was acquired for minor league pitcher Charlie Williams and an undisclosed sum of cash. The amount, estimated at $100,000 or better, is supposedly to be used by Stoneham toward the purchase of an infielder from another major league club.

In addition to "coming home," Willie also receives what amounts to more than fringe benefits. Along with his $165,000 contract, Mays was assured of both his baseball and financial future via a three-year contract that covers him as a player and as a Met employee.

Grant, chairman of the board for the Mets, said he was in no hurry to see Willie conclude his Hall of Fame career, but indicated Mays would probably work as a coach.

"He can be helpful to us and we visualize him doing the same thing Yogi did," Grant said, recalling how the current Met manager had served as a coach following his severance from the Yankees after the 1964 season.

"We're hopeful Willie will help this year and maybe even next," Grant added. "We've assured him of his baseball future, and I personally hope he's here for the rest of his life."

Mays, obviously tired but appearing relieved that his ordeal in San Francisco was over, quickly concealed any managerial aspirations he may hold. "That's Yogi's department, man," he said in his familiar high-pitched squeal. "I'm here as a player now and ready to go to work any way Yogi wants to use me."

Berra, participating briefly in the hastily concluded proceedings, said Mays would "help me in two positions—first base and the outfield."

"Yogi and I can get together and I know I can help this club," Mays said. "You know the Mets are a very good ball club and they're not going to have me playing just because I'm Willie Mays.

"I haven't played much this year, but I don't think I'll have too much trouble getting back into shape," he added. "But, as I said, it's all up to Yogi. I know I can help this ball club." ∎

M. Donald Grant, Willie Mays, and Yogi Berra talk after the trade. (News photo by Tom Cunningham.)

July 23, 1972

They're Still Great

Yogi's Number Retired

by Joe Trimble

It was heart-tugging the 26th Oldtimers' Day at the Stadium yesterday, but impressive and tastefully presented as nostalgia and sentiment filled the big, old ball park. And, true to the half-century script, the former Yankees won the abbreviated two-inning game, 4-0.

The motif was the honoring of five of the 29 World Series clubs and their fall opponents, stars from the years ending in the figure 2 being selected along with the new Hall of Famers and other greats of the past. The years were 1922, '32, '42, '52, and '62. Forget '72.

Uniform No. 8, graced by Bill Dickey and Yogi Berra down the years, was retired. Dickey was presented a replica of his uniform blouse, and Larry Berra Jr. accepted for his dad, who was in San Francisco with the Mets.

Dickey called the New York fans the "greatest in the world." Berra, speaking via a pre-recorded tape, thanked the Yanks, the fans, and also Dickey for helping his career. Yogi then drew boos when he mentioned that his absence was due to his being "with my Mets."

Tributes to those who have passed on were read as "Auld Lang Syne" was played over the PA system. Present were the widows of two of the greatest Yanks, Mrs. Babe Ruth and Mrs. Lou Gehrig.

The ceremonies were held between games of the twin bill with the Angels. ∎

President Mike Burke of the Yankees presents a No. 8 plaque to Bill Dickey (center) and uniform to Larry Berra, who represented his father, Yogi Berra, as the famed No. 8 was retired at the Stadium. (News photo by Frank Hurley.)

"You don't look so hot yourself,"
Yogi said to the Mayor's wife when she commented
on how cool Yogi looked on the hot, humid day.

In a lighter moment, Mayor John V. Lindsay honors the Mets and their manager, Yogi Berra, at a gathering on the lawn of Gracie Mansion attended by over 300. (News photo by Tom Monaster.)

"It ain't over 'til it's over."

News photo by Bill Meyer

16

1973-74: Thorny Rose

The 1973 season spawned what has become perhaps the most famous Yogiism of all time: "It ain't over 'til it's over." In mid-August, the Mets were in last place in the National League East, and many predicted that their season was over. In a heroic attempt to prove their detractors wrong, the Mets won 29 of their last 43 games to take the National League East crown.

The Mets' next task was a difficult one: they had to face Cincinnati's Big Red Machine for the National League pennant. In Game 3, the Reds' Pete Rose barreled into Bud Harrelson at second base in an attempt to break up a double play. The collision sparked a bench-clearing brawl that was still fresh in the minds of Mets fans the following June, when the Reds returned to Shea Stadium.

The Mets defeated the Reds in five games, returning to the World Series for the second time in their short history. They faced a formidable obstacle in the Oakland Athletics and were dismissed by many because of their unimpressive 82-79 regular-

season record. The Mets proved miraculous again, forcing the defending champions to seven games before finally losing the Series. ∎

Bedlam broke out when Rose crashed into Harrelson (opposite page) after Harrelson had made the pivot for his double-play throw to first. The players then exchanged blows (above), and Harrelson soon found himself headed to the ground. (News photo by Bill Meuer.)

Slide by Rose Sparks a Free-for-All

Slugs Harrelson; Fans Toss Garbage

by Dick Young

In a free-for-all so wild that one Cincy player chewed a large chunk out of a Mets cap, the Reds' manager ordered his men off the field in the midst of yesterday's play-off game, rather than subject them to a garbage shower from angry Mets fans.

Object of the cascading produce was Peter Rose, alias Charley Hustle. It was Rose's fifth-inning slide into Bud Harrelson that precipitated the ruckus. He and Buddy had a brief exchange of angry words, followed by a two-handed push by Rose, followed by a bony elbow toss by Harrelson, followed by punches—and here came everybody.

In a matter of seconds, both benches had poured onto the field. Both bullpens, too. Two bullpenners, Pedro Borbon of the Reds and Buzz Capra of the Mets, suddenly were whaling away at each other on the fringe of the main event. Players who had been trying to break up fight No. 1 turned their attention to fight No. 2, which was threatening to become a better battle.

In about five minutes, the umpires and cooler players convinced everybody it was time to leave the field. Borbon, arm-escorted by two mates, picked a baseball cap off the ground and angrily snapped it onto his head.

Take Bite out of Cap

"Hey, man," said a teammate. "That's a Met cap you have on."

Borbon whipped it off, sank his teeth into it, and yanked, ripping out a large piece. You have to be blind with rage or totally color-blind not to be able to distinguish a bright red Cincy cap from a bright blue Mets cap.

Now it was the fans' turn. As the Reds took the field, the fans in the left corner poured their refuse down upon Pete Rose. There were apples and beer cans, bottles and paper, all kinds of paper. There

After both benches cleared, Rose was pulled away from the melee by Reds coach Ted Kluszewski (l.) and catcher Johnny Bench. (News photo by Bill Meuer.)

can't be a paper shortage, and fruit must not be that expensive.

A couple of bullpenners loitered nearby. An object struck Gary Nolan, Cincy pitcher, in the face and he fell to one knee. Pete Rose picked up a bottle and flung it angrily back into the stands.

While all this was going on, the two managers and a gaggle of umpires stood at home plate arguing about who, if anybody, should be disciplined. Off to the side, at a front-row box, NL Prez Chub Feeney consulted with Commissioner Bowie Kuhn. It was decided that nobody would be ejected.

The Reds took the field for the bottom of the fifth. Koos went down on a roller. Garrett flied to left. Rose caught it—and caught hell from the fans. Somebody threw something. It grazed Rose's leg. He shouted for time out to Ed Sudol, working the left line, and started walking toward the dugout. Sparky Anderson, Cincy manager, ran out to meet him.

"I can't play with that stuff going on out there," Pete told him.

"I don't blame you." Anderson turned to the umpire. "I'm pulling my men off the field until you can guarantee their safety," he said.

Whereupon Anderson waved like a foreman calling his longshoreman off the pier. Again Feeney and Kuhn and the umpires conferred, joined by Bob Scheffing, Mets' GM, who had rushed down from his third-level box. It was decided to send a delegation of Mets players to the trouble spot to placate the fans.

Yogi, Mays Leaders

Willie Mays and Yogi Berra led the delegation, joined by Cleon Jones, Tom Seaver, and Rusty Staub. They walked to the left corner. The fans cheered. The players waved back. Willie held the peace finger aloft. The fans roared. Henry Kissinger couldn't have done better.

Some 10 minutes later, the peacemakers returned home, the Reds returned to the field, and calm was restored—for now.

The Rose-Harrelson bitterness goes back to their last picture. In yesterday's game at Cincy, after the Reds had been held to two hits by Jon Matlack, Bud Harrelson observed that Cincy's hitters had been "back on their heels."

Somebody relayed the remark to the Reds dugout. Rose bridled. "What's Harrelson, some sort of bleeping batting instructor?" he said.

And anger stays with Charley Hustle. He decided, today, to give Harrelson a sliding lesson and that's when things began to happen. ■

In brief, Yogi's a winner. Mets manager Yogi Berra looks on approvingly as Tom Seaver gives play-off hero Cleon Jones a pat on the shoulder in the Shea locker room. (News photo by Dan Farrell.)

Now You Gotta Believe in Miracles

Seaver, Kranepool, Mays, Cleon Batter the Reds, 7-2

by Phil Pepe

The miracle lives. The Mets are champions of the National League. They made it by beating the Reds, 7-2, in the sudden-death fifth game of the play-offs at Shea yesterday, a victory that touched off another crazy-mad, frenzied celebration.

Even before John Milner had tossed to Tug McGraw for the final out, they had burst loose from the barriers, these young wild fans, swarming onto the field.

It was a great victory for the Mets and most of their fans, except for that segment of maniacs whose idea of celebration was to inflict damage and discomfort.

But for the Mets, it was a great triumph, overcoming the odds and beating the powerful Reds in the best-of-five series that puts them into the World Series for the second time in their history, the first time since the first miracle of 1969.

Playing without Rusty Staub, who was out with a severely bruised right shoulder, and with Tom Seaver working with only three days of rest, the Mets pounded out 13 hits off four Reds pitchers. They broke open a 2-2 ball game with four runs in the fifth, and Seaver, who destroyed the idea that he does not win the big ones, nursed the lead into the ninth, when he needed help from McGraw, who got the last two outs.

Eddie Kranepool, a Met in every year of their existence and playing in left field for the first time since July 13 because of Staub's injury, drove in the first two runs with a single in the first.

And Willie Mays, playing the final year of his legendary career, made his first appearance since Sept. 9 as a pinch hitter in the big fifth inning. With the cheers of 50,323 still ringing in his ears, he contributed an infield single that delivered the second of the four runs.

Mets manager Yogi Berra hugs reliever Tug McGraw after McGraw shuts down Chicago to clinch the Eastern Division Championship. (News photo by Frank Hurley.)

But it was Cleon Jones' bat and Seaver's arm and guts and a mistake by a rookie third baseman that were the big items in the victory, a victory that completed a storybook year for the Mets.

Depleted of their regular team by injuries, the Mets fell 12 games off the pace in July and were 13 games under .500 in August. They got their team back in August and rallied around their beleaguered but optimistic manager Yogi Berra to come through in the National League East, a division of losers.

Winning in the lost division was one thing, the Mets were the only team to finish over .500 with a record of 82-79. Beating the Reds would be something else again. They were clearly the best team in the league, they had won 99 games, they had all those potent bats.

But the Mets had the pitching and, as Berra kept reminding everyone, pitching usually dominates a short series. Naturally, Berra was right. He usually is. ■

Downcast Rusty Told Yogi: I Can't Swing . . . I Can't Play

by Dave Hirshey

October 11, 1973—Rusty Staub got to the park early, put on the long heavy underwear that ball players wear, and couldn't wait any longer. He grabbed a bat and walked into the empty shower, and swung.

The bat moved lazily through the air, as though cutting sand. He tried it again, forced it. The shoulder hurt. He could stand the pain, but why wouldn't that damn bat move faster?

"I just couldn't swing," Staub was to say later. He reported the bad news to Yogi Berra, and went back to his locker to finish dressing.

Rusty put on a stoic appearance. He told Berra, sadly, "I can't swing . . . I can't throw . . . I can't play."

Yogi's craterlike face was wreathed in a frown as he sat on the Mets bench shaking his head. "We've come back from injuries before," Berra understated. "All season we've been catching bad breaks like this, so why should the play-offs be any different."

He smiled. Weakly. You could tell he was faking it. "You know, I really didn't think it was that serious until I watched on TV last night and saw Rusty crash into the wall in slow motion. Staub hit the hell out of that wall."

Berra said that if the Reds had been starting a southpaw it would have been Mays in right. "It might still be," he said. "If they change to a lefty, I'll change."

Somebody mentioned that the pregame odds favored the Mets, 11-10. The night before, Yogi had said he thought the Mets would be underdogs.

Yogi grinned. "If they knew Staub would be out, do you think they'd change?" he said.

October 22, 1973

A's Champs Again

by Phil Pepe

The Mets ran out of miracles here today when Bert Campaneris gathered in a soft pop fly off the bat of Wayne Garrett. The end came at 4:07 Pacific Daylight Time.

Held without a home run by superior Met pitching for six games, it was inevitable that the slugging A's, who hit 147 out of the park during the regular season, would eventually explode.

They waited until today, the sudden-death seventh game, when Campaneris and Reggie Jackson each bombed two-run homers off Jon Matlack in a four-run third to lead the A's to a 5-2 victory over the Mets that gave them the 1973 World Championship.

As inevitable as the slugging A's explosion was the fact that the Mets' inability to score runs, thereby putting tremendous pressure on their pitchers, would eventually haunt them.

They had come back here from New York, leading three games to two, and needing just one victory in two games to complete their second miracle in four years.

But they scored only three runs in the two games here and Matlack, who had not allowed an earned run in 26 innings of pressure pitching, finally faltered.

Their offensive weakness exposed, the Mets fell behind, 5-0, after five innings, an almost insurmountable lead with their bats. But to their credit, the Mets never died. They scored one run in the sixth, driving Oakland starter Ken

Holtzman out of the box for the third time, rallied in the eighth, and went down swinging in the ninth.

One run was in and the tying run was at the plate, in the person of Garrett, when Dick Williams was forced to go to his bullpen for the last time. Darold Knowles came in, setting a record by appearing in his seventh game.

The miracle was still alive. The believers kept their faith. Then Garrett hit a little pop behind short and it was fitting that Campaneris, brilliant in the entire Series, should have the honor of putting away the final out, ending the miracle. ■

The Miracle Dies —By Bill Gallo

YA GOTTA BEREAVE

Bill Gallo, Daily News, October 22, 1973

HARRELSON: WE CAME "THISCLOSE"

by Dave Hirshey

October 22, 1973—Slowly, silently, his eyes riveted on the ground in front of him, Bud Harrelson came down the narrow corridor leading to the Mets' dressing room. The sound of his spikes against the hard concrete floor made a grating noise as he suddenly stopped and turned around for one last look through the dugout onto the field that was being ravaged by deliriously happy Oakland fans.

He had to make sure that this was really happening, that the Mets had really lost, that it was not all just a horrible nightmare from which he could not wake himself. He shook his head, as though to dislodge the missed chances, the unfulfilled promise that lingered there. It was a small private gesture, but one that crystallized the disappointment of coming ever so close.

The Mets had had a remarkable year, a year in which they picked themselves up out of the depths of futility and leaped, scratched, brawled and believed their way into the World Series. But now it was over.

"It's been a helluva year for a lot of guys," said Harrelson, the brilliant shortstop who is one of those guys. But there's nothing like being No. 1. Nothing."

And the Mets finished No. 2, second best. That's why they drank Olympia beer while the A's swigged Almaden champagne. That's why they slumped in front of their lockers and stared silently at the floor while the A's danced and shouted and whooped.

"There's no compensation for finishing second," Harrelson was saying softly, the emotion beginning to creep into his voice. "They're a great ball club. All the bull they've gone through with Finley and they still go out and play for themselves. But I don't think you can say they're a better team than we are. They just played better and scored more runs."

'No Regrets' on Exit: Mays

October 22, 1973—Willie Mays had no regrets. He didn't play in his final game as an active player but he didn't want anyone singing any sad songs for him.

"I didn't want to get into the game just because I was retiring," the 42-year-old superstar said in the silent Mets dressing room.

"I didn't come in that way and I didn't want to go out that way. I don't want people feeling sorry for me."

Mays came in as a scared rookie 22 summers ago in 1951 and helped the Giants pull off one of the most improbable "Miracles" of all time as they came from $13^1/_2$ games back in August to beat the Brooklyn Dodgers in a play-off for the pennant. But Mays has lost most of the skills that enabled him to electrify baseball fans when he was the "Say Hey Kid," and announced his retirement Sept. 20.

Mays missed most of the final month with injuries. But he got one last moment of glory in the second game of this World Series when he singled in the tie-breaking run in the 12th inning with two out to start a four-run rally. That hit helped wipe out the memory of the four times Mays fell down in the game.

When Mays stripped off his uniform for the final time, he just stuffed it in his uniform bag.

"Where's your uniform?" he was asked. "I just put it in my bag," he said. "This is no time to be worrying about something like that. We just lost the Series."

Mays will continue in a capacity with the Mets for at least the next eight years at $50,000 per

October 24, 1973

Mets Tell Yogi They Believe via Three-Year Contract

by Phil Pepe

Back in July, it was a cinch the Mets would have a press conference this week to name their manager for 1974. It was less than a cinch that the man's name would be Yogi Berra.

But it was a cinch that even if he had joined the ranks of the unemployed, Berra would spend the fateful day on the golf course.

Yesterday, the Mets, without a press conference, announced that Yogi Berra had been rehired as manager of the Mets. When the announcement came, Berra was on the eighth green at the White Beeches CC in Haworth, N.J. Some things never change.

What has changed for Yogi is his tenure and his salary. He was rewarded with a three-year contract at what the Mets call a "substantial increase" and everybody else is calling $75,000 per year.

That's not bad for a guy whose future was on the rocks, his job in jeopardy, when the Mets sank to the basement of the NL East in July. His head was placed on the chopping block, rumors circulated predicting his demise, but Yogi never lost faith. He believed.

They had slipped to the bottom, through no fault of Yogi, who kept pointing out that "when we had our full team, we were in first."

Injuries depleted Berra's forces and he kept saying, "When we get our full team back, we'll be all right."

As late as Aug. 17, in last place, $7\frac{1}{2}$ games out of first, Berra told people "we can still win it." But nobody really believed.

Of course, he was right. He usually is.

When the Mets were dead-last this year in July, the fans were beginning to get restless; the rumors were starting. Berra was booed when he went to the mound to change a pitcher. Stories circulated that he would not be back next year. A poll of fans was started by one newspaper that smelled the blood of a manager.

Yogi Berra gets a key to the city from Public Events Commissioner Walter Curley as the Mighty Mets land at LaGuardia after clinching the division title in Chicago. (News photo by Charles Ruppman.)

Soon after the lowest point in their year, the lowest point in Berra's life, the team started to win. M. Donald Grant, chairman of the board, met with his players and told them, in effect, "You Gotta Believe." Grant met with Berra and told him something else.

"Don't listen to some of these crackpots," Grant said. "When this is all over with, we'll sit down and talk about next year."

Yogi agreed. This was late in the year, after the Mets started winning, when people began to say and write that Berra had done enough to be rewarded with a new contract.

Had Berra insisted on renegotiating in September, it might have cost him.

The Mets went on to win their division, then beat the Reds in the National League play-offs, and Grant was quoted as saying, "You reward a man as he produces. He's in a better bargaining position."

When others around him were losing their heads, Yogi kept his. He remained patient, he remained confident in the face of a succession of disasters.

It is said he is not tough enough, but he showed his toughness in a closed-door, put-up-or-move-out meeting with Cleon Jones, who became his best hitter in the stretch.

He stayed with Tug McGraw through hard times ("He's the best I got, I'm gonna die with him"), and McGraw saved the Mets.

It is said he's not smart enough, but Berra let Rube Walker run the pitching staff his way and, in the end, it was pitching that won for the Mets.

Now, he's got a three-year contract for $75,000 per year. Pretty dumb, that Yogi. ∎

After losing a draining seven-game Series with the World Champion Oakland A's, Yogi relaxes at the White Beeches Golf Club in Haworth, N.J. Yogi was on the eighth hole when the Mets announced his new three-year contract. (News photo by Harry Hamburg.)

Met superarm Tom Seaver and skipper Yogi Berra tell the world who they and their teammates are. They're No. 1. (News photo by Vincent Riehl.)

Yogi Berra flashes a big smile of satisfaction and Willie Mays celebrates the Mets' new division title in Willie's final season. (News photo by Frank Hurley.)

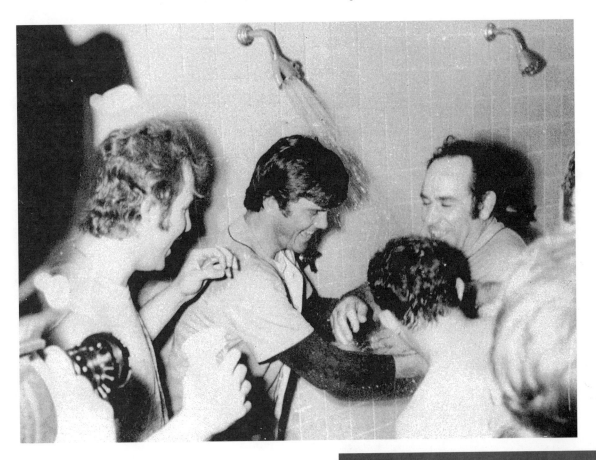

Yogi Berra (r.) who once was heading for the managerial showers, gets a bath from (l. to r.) Ken Boswell, Duffy Dyer, and Jerry Grote after the division clincher against the Cubs. (News photo by Frank Hurley.)

MISSION: IMPOSSIBLE, BUT WORTH IT. The Mets' Duffy Dyer is up against a barrage. He sees 11 baseballs being tossed out by 11 POWs at Shea. Duffy couldn't catch 'em all, not even with a basket. (News photo by Dan Farrell.)

Needing no introduction to baseball fans are Mickey Mantle, Yogi Berra, Whitey Ford, Joe DiMaggio, and Casey Stengel, all Hall of Famers, who posed before, during, and after an oldtimers' get-together at Shea Stadium. (News photo by Dan Farrell.)

OLDIES BUT GOODIES . . . Whitey Ford (l.) shows his retired number to his wife, Yogi Berra, and Mickey Mantle. Whitey and Mick were honored during Oldtimers' Day at Shea for their election to the Hall of Fame. (News photo by Anthony Casale.)

March 5, 1974—Mets GM Bob Scheffing and manager Yogi Berra discuss the upcoming season at the team's St. Petersburg, Fla. spring training camp.

Some enthusiastic (but harmless) Met fans display their opinions on Cincinnati superstar Pete Rose during the Reds' first Shea visit since last year's riot-marred NL play-offs. Rose, you remember, barreled into the Mets' Bud Harrelson at second base, sparking an all-hands brawl. Last night security was beefed up.

"Always go to other people's funerals,
otherwise they won't go to yours."

17
1975-82: Back to the Yanks

In 1975, Yogi made the return journey to the American League after 10 seasons with the Mets.

Despite his new three-year contract as the team's manager, the Mets fired him in August 1975—just midway through the contract.

As usual, Yogi seemed to roll with the punches. Before leaving the Mets clubhouse for the last time, he even set up a photo opportunity of him shaking hands with Roy McMillan, his successor, telling the photographers to "get the handshake picture."

In December, Yogi donned his familiar pinstriped number 8 jersey again when he became a member of the Yankee coaching staff under manager Billy Martin. The Yankees opened the remodeled Yankee Stadium the following April with ceremonies featuring a roster of distinguished guests, including Joe DiMaggio, Mickey Mantle, Whitey Ford, Don Larsen, Yogi, Joe Louis, Kyle Rote, Mel Allen, and even Toots Shor. The team and fans celebrated the event all year long, winning 97 games and capturing their first pennant in 10 years.

Despite the managerial turmoil that gripped the Yankees on a regular basis, Yogi was one of the constants. Amid all the changes, he remained in place as a coach for the next eight seasons. And perhaps not coincidentally, the Yankees advanced to the World Series four times during that span. ■

Looking ahead, Yogi made clear his feelings on the Mets' upcoming schedule. Little did he know that his leadership of the Mets would come to a premature end in August.

August 8, 1975

Yogi Says So Long . . . Did Best With What I Had

by Augie Borgi

When Lawrence Peter Berra woke up yesterday morning, he was still Yogi Berra, unemployed manager. More important, he was still friendly, hold-no-grudges Yogi Berra and when he left his Montclair [N.J.] home and pulled up to the toll collector on the Garden State Parkway, the toll man told me, "It's tough," and I said, "Yeah."

Even Yogi Berra had to pay the toll. Now that's important, because Yogi Berra understands his new situation: "I've been in baseball since I was 17 and I want to stay in baseball but I don't want to force myself on anybody. I don't want a job just because I'm Yogi Berra," he said.

But Yogi Berra wants a job in baseball. "Managing, I guess it's in my blood," he said at 9:30 in the morning, alone in the Met clubhouse where he would say goodbye to his players three hours later. "Sure I'd take a coaching job. Billy Martin hasn't said anything to me. No team has. I'll have to wait and see. The Mets have said I can have a job in the organization doing something. Maybe they'll want me to push a broom. Hey, you going to put that in the papers?

"I'm going to be able to play golf on Sunday for the first time during the summer in 33 years," he said. "Would I have done anything differently? No, I don't think I would. You do the best with what you have. They still got good pitching and a lot of clubs would like to have their pitching. Tate, he's going to be a good one. If you didn't start him, who would you start?"

Who the manager starts is always open to second-guessing. So Yogi knew exactly where he stood Tuesday night when the Mets were shut out twice. "I had an inkling when I was driving home, and I told Carm [his wife, Carmen]: 'I think I'm going to get a call in the morning' and I did."

So the Yog decided he had to get away. "I told Carm I wanted to go for a ride. Then I spent the afternoon just hanging around but I didn't want to talk to anybody on the phone. I took Larry [his oldest son] and some of his friends to Guido's [a restaurant] about a quarter to seven and I saw some of the game on TV when I got home. It was good for Roy to win."

Good for Roy to win. How was it for Yogi to lose?

"I tried my best so I know I did all right," he said. "My only regret is that although I won two pennants [in four tries] I didn't win the World Series [getting to the seventh game twice] so . . . that's the only thing I didn't do in baseball.

AND THEN THE LOCKER ROOM DOOR CLOSED. Even though he's wearing a trench coat, Yogi's no spy in the Mets' locker room. He's just saying so-long to the troops.

"I don't know what's going on upstairs. I heard some of the players went and complained about me. Well . . . Tom [Seaver] went upstairs . . . that's up to him. He's got his own opinions. I'm not mad at anybody, that's the way I am. I don't think many things in baseball got me mad. Maybe Phil Linz and Joe Pepitone and Cleon Jones."

Did Cleon Jones cost him his job?

"You have to ask them," Yogi said. ("I don't think so," GM Joe McDonald said. "There were so many outside things involved with Cleon. They—not Cleon—were trying to make it a racial issue. I felt Yogi did the right thing and I backed him. I thought it was time for a change of managers, though.")

"Mister Grant and I had a lot of discussions," Yogi said. About what? "No comment. I'll talk about everything you want to know. I just have to wait and see what happens. I guess I'll have to spend time with my family. It's just me and Carm in the house.

"Will I spend time mowing the lawn? Naw, it's too big. I have two acres and a 15-room house. Dale [his youngest son; in the Pirate organization] called me from Niagara Falls and I told him 'what the heck' but I didn't get to talk to Timmy [the Baltimore Colt wide receiver] 'cause he was practicing. Carm, she's relieved it's over with. I love baseball and I love New York."

Yogi pats Jerry Grote on the back as he leaves the Mets' locker room.

Cleon Gets Release

July 26, 1975—Cleon Jones has been released by the Mets, GM Joe McDonald informing the outfielder that's he's a free man at 6:30 p.m. Met manager Yogi Berra was relieved. "I wish Cleon all the luck in the world," Yogi said. "I think he wasted a lot of his talent and I believe I bent over backward to try to help him," Yogi commented. "It's not a matter of black and white. It's a matter of I wouldn't be able to face any of my players if I took him back. Like I said, I covered for Jonesy a lot. July 18th (when Jones refused to play after pinch hitting in the seventh inning) was the icing on the cake."

Then Yogi mentioned how he could have gone to Chicago ("to work for Al Lopez") and Washington ("with Gil") and St. Louis ("Red Schoendienst was looking for a coach") when the Yankees fired me but I knew I wanted to stay here. I've been in New York for 30 years."

Then he thought about coming to New York and his boyhood days in St. Louis. "My oldest brother, Tony, he would have been the best player. In an Italian family, all my father knew about baseball was it didn't pay much." Except when you make the Hall of Fame. Then Yogi went around the clubhouse, privately, saying goodbye to each player. "No speeches, I don't make speeches."

So now Yogi looked to the future. "I don't think I'll do anything this year." Then he saw Roy McMillan and a group of newspaper photographers. "Hey, get the handshake picture," Yogi ordered. Then sincerely, he shook his successor's hand. "Good luck."

Yogi went home leaving Gene Mauch, a National League manager for 16 years, to explain the state of the Mets: "I've always heard all the talk about how good the Met pitching is but the Mets will win when they have Grote, Cleon Jones, and Buddy Harrelson in good shape and playing. I don't think that will change." ∎

Pinstripe Reunion for Yogi, Cleon?

by Red Foley

Cleveland, Aug. 8, 1975—It's unlikely that Yogi Berra and Cleon Jones, baseball's newest version of the odd couple, will bring their act to the Yankees.

While Gabe Paul doesn't entirely dismiss the possibility of either joining the Yankee payroll, a reunion certainly doesn't appear imminent.

Though Paul hasn't heard from or contacted the ousted Met manager, he clearly indicated today that Yogi is not persona non grata as far as the Yankees are concerned. Neither, for that matter, is Cleon. Although Jones and the Yankees ostensibly severed their negotiations yesterday, Paul indicated his offer, on which he declined to elaborate, remained open for the present.

"How could anyone have objections to Yogi?" the Yankee president said before last night's game with Cleveland when queried on the possibility of Berra becoming a member of Billy Martin's coaching staff in 1976. Martin, when asked the same question following Yogi's Met dismissal yesterday, replied in a similar vein.

None of Martin's coaches, Elston Howard, Dick Howser, Mel Wright, or Cloyd Boyer, are signed beyond the current season. And while Martin understandably prefers not to discuss that situation at this time, baseball procedure invariably allows new managers to hire assistants of their choosing.

As for the Jones matter, Paul indicated his offer could terminate at any time. "If we were to make a player move elsewhere that would end our interest in Cleon," Paul said. "We made what we believed is a good proposition and yesterday, Jones' representative, a man named Hubert Perkins, informed me they were going to continue shopping around."

Jones, whom the Mets finally declared a free agent a week after his celebrated July 18 dugout spat with Berra at Shea, has been job-hunting the past few days. It's believed his failure to reach amicable terms with the Yankees involved a bonus payment. Apparently figuring he's a mini-Catfish Hunter, the 33-year-old, injury-plagued Jones sought front money that Paul was not willing to pay.

It's Official
Yogi and Yanks Back Together

by Red Foley

December 6, 1975—Yogi will be on display when the refurbished Yankee Stadium opens for business next year. So, too, will holdover coaches Elston Howard and Dick Howser. But Whitey Ford, the ailing pitching coach, won't be a member of manager Billy Martin's staff.

According to Martin, who participated via a conference call from Hilton Head, S.C., Howard and Howser will continue as first- and third-base coaches, respectively, with Yogi assisting Martin from the dugout.

Berra, who said he didn't know if he would ever try managing again, expressed happiness at returning to the Yankees. The fact they fired him after he won the 1964 pennant had no apparent effect on Yogi.

"After all, it's a whole new regime since I was there before," he said.

Flashing his infectious grin, Yogi Berra displays his pinstripes at the Americana Hotel, where it was announced that he's returning to the Yankees. As coach, he'll wear his familiar No. 8, retired to honor Yogi and Bill Dickey, who both wore it with Hall of Fame distinction. Yogi will be on hand when the Yanks open the new Stadium, hopefully the same way they christened its predecessor—with a championship. (News photo by Dan Farrell.)

April 15, 1976

Infield a Bit Wavy but New Stadium Stunning

by Phil Pepe

Workmen were hammering away, putting rubber padding on the inside roof of the Yankee dugout, a precaution against some excited player standing straight up and conking his head on a slab of concrete. Electricians worked against the clock to install sufficient lighting for the opening game, just hours away. The pitcher's mound was too low, the infield too wavy, the scoreboard clock was 14 minutes slow, there were empty cartons in the home team's clubhouse, the sauna did not work, and there was no carpet in the manager's office.

Still and all, remodeled Yankee Stadium is a beautiful ball park, a showplace that combines the charm of the old and the conveniences of the new, and it will open, ready or not, this afternoon when the Yankees meet the Twins sometime after 2 o'clock amid a whole lot of pomp and ceremony, thereby ending a two-year road trip.

"It's the sharpest park in the league, without a doubt," Billy Martin decided. "It's even prettier than those new parks. I just hope it has the same number of wins it used to have, like about 104."

There is much work to be done, inside and out, but when it is all finished Yankee Stadium, two years in the rebuilding, a $100 million palace of which $55 million was spent improving the neighborhood and roads, will be a sight to behold. It is already, with its white exterior and blue interior, its modern scoreboard with telescreen for instant replay (not operating today because of technical difficulties), its unobstructed view from all seats, its escalators and Hall of Fame Plaza. Its baseball-shaped boiler stack. Its parking for 7,000 cars.

Yogi Berra, Billy Martin, and Elston Howard christen the new Yankee Stadium.

A capacity crowd of 34,028 is expected to be on hand with the weatherman favoring the opening with springlike temperatures in the high 60s, and the beauty of the stadium will make all the kinks tolerable.

The ground crew worked until the wee hours and was on the job again at 7 this morning working on the field. Although surveyors measured the mound at the regulation 10 inches in height, the Yankees had Catfish Hunter throw off it at yesterday's workout. What the Catfish wanted the Catfish would get—within the rules, of course.

"The[y] must have graded this field in a rowboat," said Yogi Berra, noting the sloping of the infield and the outfield.

"It's terrible," said third baseman Graig Nettles. "But there's nothing the ground crew can do until we go away on our next long road trip. Until then, we'll just have to play on it as it is. The infield's wavy, but the park is beautiful."

Lou Piniella shrugged when it was pointed out that right field sloped upward and if a ball was hit to the fence, the right fielder would be running up the hill.

"So what," said sweet Lou. "I've been running uphill all my life."

The outfield dimensions have been reduced in left center and right, and left fielder Roy White said it felt strange to stand in left and look in at the plate.

"I didn't know where I was at," Roy said. "I can't gauge the distance out there yet."

There were other things about the park that were strange. Landmarks and signposts that were there before are gone now. Exits and entrances you once knew are not exits or entrances anymore.

"I got lost coming into our clubhouse," said Elston Howard, who first walked into Yankee Stadium in 1955. And he was not alone.

But the end result is magnificent and, it will open at noon today, and at 1:32 ceremonies will begin. Great moments in Yankee Stadium history will be recalled, with introductions of Joe DiMaggio, Mickey Mantle, Whitey Ford, Don Larsen, Yogi Berra, Frank Gifford, Kyle Rote, Joe Louis, Glenn Davis, Doc

Starting Lineups
Opening Day 1976
New Yankee Stadium

TWINS	YANKEES
Terrell, 2b	*Rivers, cf*
Ford, rf	*White, lf*
Carew, 1b	*Munson, c*
Hisle, cf	*Chambliss, 1b*
Kusick, dh	*Nettles, 3b*
Wynegar, c	*Gamble, rf*
McKay, 3b	*Randolph, 2b*
Brye, lf	*Coggins, dh*
Thompson, ss	*Mason, ss*
Goltz, p	*May, p*

Bianchard, Johnny Lujack, and all living members of the 1923 Yankees, the first team to call Yankee Stadium home.

Bobby Richardson will read the invocation. Robert Merrill will sing the national anthem and four special guests will be introduced—former Postmaster General James A. Farley; restaurateur Toots Shor; longtime Yankee clubhouse custodian Pete Sheehy; and longtime voice of the Yankees Mel Allen.

Bob Shawkey, starting pitcher when the stadium opened for the first time, will throw out the first ball. And then it will be "Play Ball" in the most famous baseball park of them all—still majestic, still stately, still exciting, but all dressed up now with a brand-new facelift. ∎

A familiar scene during Yogi's coaching tenure with the Yankees—celebrating American League pennants and World Series Championships with owner George Steinbrenner and manager Billy Martin. From 1976 through 1981, Yogi and the Yankees appeared in the World Series four times, winning twice. (News photo courtesy of Dan Farrell.)

YANKEES' WORLD SERIES APPEARANCES
1976-81

1976	Cincinnati Reds over Yankees 4-0	
	Manager—Billy Martin	
1977	Yankees over L.A. Dodgers 4-2	
	Manager—Billy Martin	
1978	Yankees over L.A. Dodgers 4-2	
	Manager—Bob Lemon	
1981	L.A. Dodgers over Yankees 4-2	
	Manager—Bob Lemon	

THREE PITCHES, THREE SWINGS, THREE HOME RUNS.
Reggie Jackson's heroics in Game 6 of the 1977
World Series confirmed his place in baseball history
as "Mr. October."

Ron Guidry's 1978
season will be
remembered as
one of the
greatest
performances of
any pitcher in
baseball history.
He was 25-3 with a
1.74 ERA, and
earned the AL Cy
Young Award. His
hitting, however,
was limited to the
occasional World
Series sacrifice.

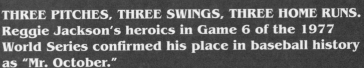

Although Dave Winfield struggled (1-22) in
the 1981 World Series, he went on to lead the
Yankees throughout the 1980s. Starring at
the plate and in the field, Winfield appeared
in 12 All-Star games and won seven Gold
Gloves during his career.

NOW THAT'S ITALIAN! The weather was sparkling and the music stirring as 100,000 marchers paraded up Fifth Ave. yesterday in the annual Columbus Day parade. The Italian-born mariner was saluted both by Italian-Americans and American-Italians-for-a-day. Amid the adulation, the parade's grand marshal, Yogi Berra, expressed the general sentiment: "I'm glad my father came over." (News photo by Harry Hamburg.)

Nonvocal coach Yogi Berra compares grip with diva Eleanor Steber. Mrs. Yogi (Berra) is at left. (News photo by Gene Kappock.)

Yogi on Entertainment

"I really liked it. Even the music was good."

Yogi commented after he and Carmen saw the opera, Tosca.

"Only the scary parts," he responded.

During his stint as a movie critic, Yogi was asked if the movie
Fatal Attraction had frightened him.

"What's wrong with him now?"

Yogi asked Carmen after she said she took their son Tim to see Dr. Zhivago.

"He must have made that movie before he died,"

Yogi said about Steve McQueen's 1968 movie Bullitt.

"Well, who's in it?"

Yogi replied when asked whether he wanted to see an X-rated movie.

"I wish I had a answer to that because I'm tired of answering that question."

18

1983-85: A Vote of Confidence???

In December 1983, after firing Billy Martin for the third time in six years, George Steinbrenner appointed Yogi as the new Yankee manager.

During the 1984 season, Yogi generated a storm of controversy when he moved pitcher Dave Righetti from the starting rotation to the bullpen, making him the Yankees' closer. By the time the season ended, so had the controversy—Righetti racked up 31 saves, despite missing a number of games with a finger injury.

Another Berra joined the Yankees after the 1984 season: in December, commissioner Peter Ueberroth approved a trade between the Yankees and Houston that brought Dale, the youngest of Yogi and Carmen's three sons, to New York to play for his father. Despite questions about the advisability of a father managing his son, the Berras were convinced that they could make the situation work.

Unfortunately, they never had a chance to find out. Contrary to his assurances throughout spring training and the early days of the season, Steinbrenner continued his game of musical managers. On April 28, he replaced Yogi with Billy Martin, the man dubbed the "human boomerang." Among Yankee players and fans the move brought on a new wave of contempt for Steinbrenner and an outpouring of support for Yogi. ■

Yogi Berra at a Yankee Stadium press conference naming him as the new manager of the Yankees succeeding Billy Martin. (News photo by Dan Farrell.)

December 17, 1983

Boss' Ax Finally Falls As Yogi Replaces Billy

By Bill Madden

The long-expected, much-delayed Yankee manager switch at last became official yesterday when George Steinbrenner pushed his revolving door once again and ushered in Yogi Berra to replace Billy Martin.

When asked if he had considered Berra as a manager for a while, Steinbrenner acknowledged he had actually offered the job to Yogi on a couple of occasions in the past, only to be turned down. Why did Berra – who has been given a two-year contract – accept this time?

"My age had something to do with it," Yogi replied. "I've achieved just about everything a man can achieve in this game. I've won the Most Valuable Player award, I've made the Hall of Fame and I've won two pennants as a manager. But I've never won a (world) championship (as a manager). I felt that this club is capable of winning one. In the past, when George talked to me about the job, I didn't really know the players that well. But I think I know these guys real well and I think they can win."

Considering Steinbrenner's penchant for pushing his own ideas and suggestions on his managers, the low-keyed Berra might well be the perfect choice this time. "I don't care what he does," Yogi said of Steinbrenner. "That don't bother me. I don't get mad. I listen. I always believed four heads are better than one."

As for Martin, Steinbrenner said: "I'm shifting people around. Nobody is leaving. I'm doing what's necessary for everybody's best interests, not just mine and Billy's but for the team's too. Those are decisions that have to be made and I made them."

More and more it has become apparent that about the best job in baseball is to become one of

Steinbrenner's ex-managers. Perhaps that was why Berra did not insist on anything more than two years.

"I'll argue with George about things probably," Berra conceded, "and then I'll find out, I guess, whether I can win one. But I can accept losing an argument, too. Why did I want only two years? I might want to retire after that. I just hope George takes care of me, too."■

It Should Be A Lot Quieter

December 17, 1983—The Yankee clubhouse, a scene of unrest and confusion most of last year, is likely to be a much more tranquil place next year under Yogi Berra. At least that was the subtle message yesterday coming from the Yankee players in the wake of Billy Martin's departure.

"I think everybody knew my situation with Billy," said Steve Kemp, whose agent reportedly asked for a trade if Martin came back. "I just wasn't able to communicate with Billy."

"How can you not bust your butt for Yogi?" asked Rick Cerone, another Yankee who quickly fell into Martin's disfavor last season. "Last year we had a lot of conflicts of interest in the clubhouse."—Madden

Easy-Going Yogi Won't Be Pushover

The Yankees should not be fooled by Yogi's easy-going demeanor. People who were around the Yanks in '64 when Yogi last managed pinstripes still recall the day he backed Roger Maris up against the clubhouse wall to assert his authority. Maris had allegedly tried to show Yogi up after being removed from an exhibition game. It was the first and last time Yogi and "The Rog" ever clashed as Maris was one of the real "gamers" for the Yankees . . . Don't be surprised, by the way, if one of Yogi's first moves is to send Ken Griffey back to center field (gimpy knees allowing) so that Don Mattingly can be in the lineup at first base every day.

—Bill Madden

Yogi Berra and Mickey Mantle were among Yank greats on hand last night to greet Roger Maris (l.), Pride of the Yankees Award winner at the team's homecoming dinner. (News photo by Vincent Riehl.)

YANKEES' BILLY-GATE REVOLVES, AGAIN

George Steinbrenner's Revolving Door of Managers since 1973:

1974	**Names Bill Virdon to succeed Ralph Houk, who resigned after '73 season.**
Aug. 1, 1975:	**Fires Bill Virdon and replaces him with Billy Martin.**
July 25, 1978:	**Names Bob Lemon to replace Billy Martin who resigned under pressure.**
June 18, 1979:	**Fires Bob Lemon and replaces him with Billy Martin.**
December 1979:	**Fires Billy Martin and replaces him with Dick Howser.**
Nov. 21, 1980:	**Fires Dick Howser and replaces him with Gene Michael.**
Sept. 6, 1981:	**Fires Gene Michael and replaces him with Bob Lemon.**
April 25, 1982:	**Fires Bob Lemon and replaces him with Gene Michael.**
Aug. 3, 1982:	**Fires Gene Michael and replaces him with Clyde King.**
Jan. 11, 1983:	**Replaces Clyde King with Billy Martin.**
Dec. 16, 1983:	**Fires Billy Martin and replaces him with Yogi Berra.**

Dale-Yogi: Will It Be Berrable?

by Phil Pepe

Yogi Wisdom

"If he hits, he plays. If he don't hit, he sits."—Yogi on Dale

Dale Berra is not the first major league baseball player to be managed by his father. But Earle Mack and *his* father, Connie, have long since shed their mortal coils. So the search for insight into the unusual situation facing Dale, the Yankee third baseman, and Yogi, his father and manager, leads to the person who knows the principals best.

"I don't think there will be any problem; the only problem will be in the minds of other people," said Carmen Berra.

That might not be the most objective opinion, because Carmen Berra is the wife of the manager and the mother of the third baseman. But she also has observed about 3,000 baseball games in the past 35 springs, summers, and autumns, and that must count for something.

"You have to know the individuals involved," Carmen said. "You have to know that with Yogi, the most important thing is the team. Winning comes first, and he's not going to favor Dale at the expense of the team just because he's his son.

"And you have to know Dale. He idolizes his father. He is not going to do anything to jeopardize Yogi's job."

The reasoning is flawless, but skeptics abound and questions persist.

What will happen when Dale is benched and thinks he should be playing?

What will the other players think if Dale is not hitting and the manager keeps him in the lineup?

Will Dale's teammates be reluctant to criticize the manager in front of him because they fear what they say will get back to Yogi?

December 21, 1984—Dale Berra gives a new dimension to the infield Pop rule. (News photo by Dan Farrell.)

"It's not a good situation," said one veteran baseball man who requested anonymity. "It presents too many problems. I don't think it can work."

Others prefer to take a wait-and-see attitude, largely because of Yogi's personality. The feeling is that this man is so aboveboard that if anyone can handle managing his own son, Yogi can.

"It will be tougher on the son than the father," said Dodger VP Al Campanis, whose son, Jim, was a catcher in the Dodger organization. "I was always tougher on my own son than I was on the other players. One spring, I found out he came in late one night and I really chewed his butt. Twenty-six other guys also came in late, but he was the one who heard about it. And if something happened in the clubhouse and I found out about it, people suspected I heard it from my son."

Perhaps it's the Ripkens who can best understand the situation faced by the Berras. The father, Cal Sr., is an Oriole coach. The son, Cal Jr., is the Orioles' star shortstop.

"It's not the same as managing my son," said Cal Sr., "but there are no problems. He goes his way; I go mine. He does his job; I do mine. If we want to have dinner together, we do it. After all, he is my son."

It is this sort of up-front attitude that characterizes Yogi and Dale. With his gift for simplifying complex things, Yogi explains how he will handle Dale: "If he hits, he plays. If he don't hit, he sits."

And Dale proves he is a chip off the old block when asked how he intends to address his father.

"I'm not going to call him 'Skip,'" said Dale. "That would be silly. I'll call him what I've always called him. 'Dad.' Who am I kidding? Everybody knows he's my father."

Dale is the youngest of the three Berra sons. Because of the nature of his work, Yogi was an absentee father to Larry Jr., Tim, and Dale, but the quality time he spent with his boys more than compensated for any lack of quantity time. Yogi did not change diapers when the boys were infants, and he always had a difficult time being the disciplinarian of the family.

"That was my job," said Carmen. "You know how easygoing Yogi is, but if he ever got angry, the boys knew enough to behave. Yogi has been the greatest influence on the boys. They idolize their father. They have always had a great time together. When the boys were little, Yogi would play touch football with them or you'd see him on the living-room floor, wrestling with them."

These days, Yogi and his sons are together frequently at family gatherings. When dinner is over, they might play Trivial Pursuit or watch home movies or talk about sports. All sports.

"I have had no influence on them whatsoever," said Carmen. "After all, I'm just a woman."

She is a woman who has had the qualities to be father and mother to her children during her husband's absences. Her job has been more difficult than she admits.

Now, with the wisdom of her years and the perspective of having seen the interaction between father and son, she is certain this new relationship between manager and player will work.

"I thought getting Dale was great," she said. "Not just because he's our son. They wanted an infielder and Dale is a good player. He's not a superstar, but he's a solid player. I think we need him.

"Dale feels perfectly comfortable being on a team managed by his father. He's 100 percent secure. If he has a complaint, he'll go to his father, just as he went to Chuck Tanner in Pittsburgh. And if his teammates are concerned that he will run back and tell his father everything he hears, he'll try to change their mind. But he's not going to worry about it.

"I know this: if Yogi is fired and Dale is still there, he'll play as hard for the next manager as he does for his father." ■

"Our similiarities are different," Dale told *Sports Illustrated* when comparing himself to his father.

February 26, 1985

Righetti Breathes a Sigh of Relief

by Bill Madden

Ft. Lauderdale—On a pitching staff riddled with question marks, the one question fans, reporters, and Yankee opponents alike will never stop asking no longer even requires an answer.

Ask any of the principals involved whether there are any circumstances in which Dave Righetti might yet be returned to a starting role, and watch the reaction.

With the man himself, Righetti, it's a rolling of the eyes upward. With the manager, Yogi Berra, it's a smile and a shake of the head. With the general manager, Clyde King, it's an exasperated throwing of the hands and arms upward.

"What more can I say other than the first time out Rags saved me 31 games. Who knows how many more he might have had if he hadn't missed 15 with that finger injury!" Berra said. "And all those 31 saves were legit because we were very careful to use him only in 'game' situations. You just can't find quality short relievers like that."

"Last year, when the most pressure was being put on Yogi to move Righetti back to the starting rotation, it was because Dave wasn't getting enough save opportunities early on," added King. "Well, if we'd have had Sutter, he'd have been in the same position."

"As I said last year," Berra continued, "if I made Rags a starter again, who would save him?"

Righetti understands—and now accepts. There are still some reservations that, he admits, will always be there.

Manager Yogi Berra greets Dave Righetti (r.), coming in to relieve Phil Niekro (l.) during the Yanks' 5-1 win vs. the White Sox.

"I take a lot of pride in being the guy who takes the weight off everybody else on the staff," Righetti said. "I enjoyed being the one they all counted on last year. I wouldn't want to be switched back now. It was the principle of the matter that gave me reservations. This is a career move and I can't help but think of my younger brother who had a chance to play one more year of professional ball and decided to quit. He'll never get that back now. I guess what I'm saying is that I needed to tap out as a starter."

Because it *was* a career move and because he did it without complaint, it was thought the Yankee high command would make an effort this winter to show their appreciation by revising Righetti's $2.2 million contract (signed in 1983), which extends through 1986 with an option for '87.

"To tell you the truth, I would have been surprised if I did hear from them," said Righetti. "I'm not complaining. They gave me a good contract." ∎

Give Yogi Some Credit

April 21, 1985—Isn't it time all those who criticized Yogi Berra for putting Dave Righetti in the bullpen admit that the Yankee manager was right? In the Yanks' first four wins, Righetti had a victory and three saves. What would he have had as a starter? Maybe one victory, or none, with no Righetti to protect the lead. Who's to say Righetti would be a sure 20-game winner as a starter? In his best year, he won only 14 (completing 7-of-31 starts) and he had Goose Gossage behind him. Righetti, who had frequent arm problems as a starter, has been sound as a reliever. Besides, even if he could win 20 as a starter, I'd rather have a guy who can save 40.—Phil Pepe

Yogi strikes his familiar pose as manager on the Yankee bench.

February 21, 1985

Steinbrenner Says Yogi's Job Is Safe for the 1985 Season

by Bill Madden

Ft. Lauderdale—There will be no axe nor even a Billy Martin or an Earl Weaver hanging over Yogi Berra's head this year even if—heaven forbid!—the Yankees should stumble out of the American League starting gate again and fall out of the race before it has begun.

So decreed George Steinbrenner yesterday—in much the same fashion as he did a year ago. And, as we all remember, The Boss stuck to his word on Yogi last year even if there were some anxious moments last June when Martin was poised and ready to reassume the field command of the Yankees.

Steinbrenner did not even wait for the first Yankees to begin assembling here to issue his surprise vote of confidence. The Boss showed up at Ft. Lauderdale Stadium and, upon being confronted for the coming season, responded:

"Yogi will be the manager this year, period. I said the same thing last year and I stuck to my word. A bad start will not affect Yogi's status either. In the past I have put a lot of pressure on my managers to win at certain times. That will not be the case this spring."

Steinbrenner also said he would not be concerned with the Yankees' won-lost record in spring training either—another out-of-character posture for him.

"I'm not going to worry if we lose a game to Boston or the Mets [in spring training]," he said. "We've got some players we want to take a look at and that's what we're going to get done."

Berra was understandably pleased with his early vote of confidence, but perhaps remembering, too, that Bob Lemon was told the same thing in 1982 (only to be fired two weeks into the season), he was taking it all very cautiously.

"We had our meeting here Tuesday night and it went very well," Berra said. "He [Steinbrenner] told me not to worry about spring training. Just worry about the season. That doesn't mean I'm not gonna win as many games as I can down here. This helps, though. It lets me manage with a clear mind." ■

Yankee owner George Steinbrenner issues his vote of confidence to manager Yogi Berra before the 1985 season.

April 26, 1985

Boss Buries Hatchet, Doesn't Hatchet Berra

by Paul Needell

A few reporters slinked into the manager's office in the Yankee clubhouse three hours before last night's game with the Boston Red Sox. They tried to act as if they weren't surprised to find Yogi Berra sitting behind the desk.

"All I know is that I'm still here," Berra shrugged. The phrase "for now," although unspoken, hovered over the room. "He [Guess Who?] must think we don't have feelings, too. We don't like losing, either."

The Yankees had lost three straight games before last night's 5-1 victory over the Red Sox, and had committed 14 errors in their last seven games. Most managers would not be feeling the heat so early in the season, but then, George Steinbrenner is not most owners. "Everyone is saying if he doesn't win tonight, he's out tonight. That's not the case," said George.

If Steinbrenner does replace Berra, his first choice is former Baltimore manager Earl Weaver. However, Weaver had not indicated any great desire to return to managing at this point in time, and told Steinbrenner exactly that in a phone conversation April 12.

Anyway, Yogi's status appears safe for at least one more game. Further updates will have to come from the prodigious mouthings of Steinbrenner, who did not attend last night's game, but is expected to join the club in Chicago this weekend.

"No question, the guys are playing uptight," designated hitter Don Baylor said. "They're trying to do more than they're capable of. And it's all for the manager. It would be different if it was a manager here who nobody respected or gave a damn about. Losing is hurting us, but nobody in this room is hurting more than Yogi. And we realize that." ■

When Yogi was asked if Don Mattingly's All-Star play had exceeded his expectation, Yogi replied, "He's done more than that."

April 29, 1985

Billy Replaces Yogi

Yankee Players Infuriated by Move

by Bill Madden

Chicago—In a script that is all too familiar in the dizzy, daffy world of George Steinbrenner's Yankees, Yogi Berra was fired as manager yesterday after 16 games of the season and Billy Martin was named to take charge for the fourth time, joining the team today in Texas.

Yankee players reacted with anger and bitterness upon learning the news. Don Baylor, a critic of the way Martin handled the club during his stormy last term in 1983, glanced at the news release, then picked up a trash container and heaved it across the room, scattering debris throughout the clubhouse. Don Mattingly reacted in similar fashion, slamming bowls around in the trainer's room.

Later, when Berra emerged from his office and began going from player to player, shaking hands for the last time, he was embraced by a red-eyed Mattingly.

Only Rickey Henderson, a Martin favorite from the days when they were together in Oakland, greeted the news with open happiness. But as Henderson smiled and chuckled about the prospect of once again playing for Martin, other veteran Yankees—Mattingly, Baylor, Dave Winfield, and Ken Griffey—glared at him.

The end came for Berra after the White Sox had completed a three-game sweep of the Yankees with a 4-3 triumph that was decided when Joe Cowley issued a two-out, bases-loaded walk to rookie Ozzie Guillen in the bottom of the ninth inning. But the cruelest irony of all for Berra was that former Yankee Oscar Gamble tied the score with a two-run homer in the seventh inning. Berra had fought bitterly for Gamble's release this past winter over Steinbrenner's wishes.

According to Yankee general manager Clyde King, who informed Berra of his dismissal during a private meeting in the visiting manager's office, Steinbrenner had made up his mind to make the change before yesterday's game.

"I knew about it during the game," King said. "Mr. Steinbrenner said he had hoped Yogi could have gone out on a winner."

If he was hurt or bitter, though, Berra did not show it.

"What do you guys need?" a smiling Berra said to the mob of reporters around him. "All you need is a headline that says, 'Yogi is fired.' I have no regrets. I don't think my players laid down on me and tried to lose, and I still think this club will come around.

"But he [Steinbrenner] is the boss and I'm used to it. This is three times for me [Berra was dismissed by the Yanks in 1964 and by the Mets in 1975]. That's the way this game is. My contract doesn't say I have to do anything if I'm fired, so I'm going to go home and play golf."

Pitcher John Montefusco was one of many players upset by the firing of Berra, who had replaced Martin as manager in December 1983. "This is the hardest thing for me to take," he said. "Yogi was a friend to everyone, but it wasn't Yogi's fault. Nothing surprises me anymore."

Said Joe Cowley, yesterday's losing pitcher: "Yogi showed he had a lot of confidence in me. He made me a better pitcher. I'm going to miss him. Shame, isn't it?"

Third baseman Dale Berra, Yogi's son, first refused comment, then said, "That's the way the game is today."

It should be remembered that Steinbrenner, on the first day of spring training this year, grabbed back-page headlines by pronouncing that Berra was safe for the entire season, "no matter what."

But after the season began and the Yankees lost three straight to the Boston Red Sox in their opening series, Steinbrenner gradually recanted that vote of confidence. ■

Grim Flight Aboard Air Boss

by Bill Madden

Arlington, Tex., April 30, 1985—*Conspicuous on the somber Yankee plane flight from Chicago to Dallas Sunday night was the empty seat in the first row next to Clyde King.*

"This whole thing didn't really hit me until I sat down here next to this seat where Yogi always was," said King, the Yankee general manager.

It was apparent that the sudden but not unexpected firing of Yogi Berra had not really hit the Yankee players, either. There was very little talk on the flight, not even the usual discussion of what might be expected by a new manager.

Most of these Yankees know what to expect from Billy Martin and it was evident they did not relish the prospect of playing for him again.

"I want you to know," said Joe Cowley to the traveling writers, "I feel lousy. I feel real lousy."

He was referring to the game-ending, bases-loaded walk he had issued to Chicago White Sox shortstop Ozzie Guillen that made Berra's final game as Yankee manager a 4-3 loss. Later, though, Cowley, who was not with the Yankees when Martin last managed them in 1983, became inquisitive about the new manager.

"What can I expect?" Cowley asked.

"Expect to throw strikes," said Don Baylor.

Otherwise, most of the players looked grim and talked quietly among themselves. They seemed overcome by a sense of sadness that they had let down a manager they had all genuinely liked and respected. There was also an underlying mood of disbelief that Yankee owner George Steinbrenner had fired Berra after only 16 games.

"This is just unbelievable," said one player. "You have to wonder if he's gone over the brink."

Up in the front of the plane, King, Berra's closest friend and confidant throughout Yogi's 178-game second go-round as Yankee manager, sat alone with his thoughts. In his own delicate tenure as Steinbrenner's man for all positions, King had always been a willing brunt of jokes about his voracious appetite. But when the stewardess began passing out the dinner, he looked up from his notebook and said quietly: "No, thank you. Not for me. I'm not hungry."

Yogi Comes Home

He's Gone From Yankees, but the Spirit Lives On

by Mike Lupica

The three blue bleacher seats were on the porch that sat in the shade on the left side of the big house on Highland Road in Montclair. Behind them in the distance, across the Hudson River, was the skyline of Manhattan. The bleacher seats were from the old Yankee Stadium, the real one. They had some mileage on them and needed a new coat of paint. They were, in fact, a lot like the man who owned them, and owned the stately gray-blue house. Yogi Berra is a little worn right now, a little tired looking, and he has seen better days, but he is still the Yankees. The man who fired him cannot take that away from him. Yogi Berra sat in the middle bleacher seat and lit a Lucky Strike. He was asked if he was angry about losing his job.

"What's the use of getting angry," he said in the familiar croak, trying to open up his closed fist of a face into a smile. "I did the best I can and the players did, too."

He wore a Lacoste sweater the color of the sky and brown slacks and beige shoes. It was a little past four in the afternoon. He had driven to Yankee Stadium in the morning to clean out his office—"didn't take long, I don't have that much stuff"—and come home to Jersey and hit some practice golf balls at the Montclair Golf Club a few miles from his home.

"Then I was gonna come home for good." A car stopped on the street and a man got out and yelled, "We're still with you, Yogi." The man spoke for Yankee fans. Yogi waved at him. The man got into his car and drove off.

It was mentioned to Yogi how much the game has changed, how much a joke the Yankees have become under a principal owner who evaluates his managers inning by inning and worries about the Mets the way Queeg worried about missing strawberries. Yogi tossed the softball to his grandson again and smiled finally.

"Yeah," he said, "but it's still a pretty good game, isn't it?"

He was asked if he would continue to work for the Yankees in some capacity and he said, "Gotta think about that" and he was asked if he would come back for Oldtimers Day and he paused before saying, "Gotta think about that one, too." Maybe the princi-

YOGI SHOWS UP AT SHEA

by Jack Lang

May 2, 1985—Yogi Berra can't stay away from baseball. Just three days after he was relieved of his job as Yankee manager, Yogi showed up at Shea Stadium last night to watch the Mets play the Astros.

Yogi and his wife, Carmen, were guests of Houston owner Dr. John J. McMullen at dinner in the Shea Director's Room before the game and then watched the action from Mets owner Nelson Doubleday's enclosed luxury box.

Yogi, who had resumed smoking during his hectic spring with the Yankees, says he will give up cigarettes again starting Sunday. Other than to pose for a picture with McMullen outside the Doubleday box, the deposed Yankee manager had nothing to say.

pal owner has done that; maybe he has run Yogi off Oldtimers Day. Yogi said he had spoken to the Yankees' principal owner after the firing Sunday: "It was nothin' much. Just a phone call." Yesterday afternoon Yogi called Billy Martin in Texas and wished him luck.

"I told him we got a hell of a team, and we're gonna snap out of it," Yogi said. It is the same message he had given his players Sunday afternoon as he shook their hands and said goodbye.

Carmen came out of the house and talked about dragging her husband to Europe in the summer for a golfing tour that would start at St. Andrew's in Scotland. Yogi and Carmen worried out loud that granddaughter Lindsey, who is scheduled to make her First Communion on Sunday, had already caught the chicken pox from Lawrence III. The two daughters-in-law said they would be back in time for dinner. The little grandson tired of the softball and found himself a blue toy airplane. "He don't have much of an arm yet," Yogi said.

It looked like a normal day at the Berra home on Highland Road, but it was not a normal day, because the only real baseball in it would be played on television, and another man would be managing Yogi Berra's team. The Yankee bleachers seats were on the porch, but the baseball season was a million miles away. After 42 years, Yogi had a day off. ∎

Yogi's day off had something missing. (News photo by Bill Turnbull.)

Dale Shaken by Dad's Firing
by Bill Madden

Chicago, April 29, 1985—Of all the visibly stunned and angered Yankee players yesterday, no one was hit harder by the firing of Yogi Berra than Dale Berra.

"He took it with class, like the real man that he is," said Dale of his father. With tears in his eyes, Dale told of his meeting with his father.

"He told me not to feel bad for him—that his time is passed now but the future is all mine. I feel awful, but I also felt very proud watching him go around the clubhouse shaking hands with every player and seeing how they reacted."

SUDDENLY BASEBALL IS FUN AGAIN. Lawrence Peter Berra, the squire of Montclair, N.J., has a game of catch with grandson, Larry, as his wife, Carmen (shading eyes), and daughters-in-law, Betsy and Leigh, admire the young athlete's form. When led around to his firing, Yogi said with irrefutable logic: "What's the use of getting angry? I did the best I can and the players did too." (News photo by Bill Turnbull.)

Yogi Berra, rid of the pressures of managing the Yankees, relaxes in an old Yankee Stadium bleacher seat yesterday in his backyard. (News photo by Bill Turnbull.)

November 27, 1985

Half-Baked Idea Will Aid Poor

by Richard Sisk

Math quiz: If it takes the Transit Authority 16 years to build a tunnel to Queens and it isn't finished yet, how long will it take Yogi to fungo 23 tons of potatoes off his lawn?

Luckily, this problem will remain unsolved, since everybody's favorite catcher-manager-philosopher is giving the spuds to charity, minus a box or two for his family and neighbors in Montclair, N.J.

The latest chapter in the continuing adventures of Yogi began last year at a charity golf tournament in Fargo, N.D., hometown of ex-Yankee Roger Maris. The tournament was sponsored by the American Cancer Society. Maris is suffering from the disease.

It seems that Yogi was told that potatoes were a big crop out there, and the Hall of Famer responded: 'You don't have enough potatoes to fill my front lawn."

Yogi couldn't remember saying that exactly, but it was enough for the Red River Valley Potato Growers Association.

A big truck with a banner reading "The Red River Valley and Yogi Go to Bat for the Needy" showed up in front of Yogi's house at 8 a.m. yesterday and began unloading on his lawn.

"Yogi, what are you doing to us this morning?" a neighbor yelled. "Come back later, Virginia, and get some potatoes," Berra answered.

The bulk of the potatoes will be delivered in Yogi's name to the Hunts Point Cooperative Farmers' Market in the Bronx and eventually will reach food banks for the needy. ∎

It's over: Yogi Berra carts away the last box of potatoes dumped on his Montclair lawn. (News photo by Anthony Casale.)

"I don't know. I'm not in shape yet," Yogi answered when asked his cap size as he checked into the clubhouse as a coach for the Houston Astros.

19

1986-89: Destination Houston

After he was fired by Steinbrenner, Yogi decided not to manage again, but he had one more destination on his tour of duty in professional baseball. He joined the Houston Astros as a member of rookie manager Bob Lanier's staff in November 1985. Once again, Yogi looked to the future, refusing to dwell on past problems.

In addition to his coaching and managerial experience, Yogi brought to Houston his sense of humor and an intangible tendency toward success and good fortune. This factor, known as "Yogi Luck," was even credited with steering the Astros to the National League West title in 1986.

Yogi spent four seasons in a multi-colored Astros uniform, wearing his familiar number 8. The move was a significant change of venue for Yogi and Carmen, as it was the only time since his major league debut that he worked for a baseball team that did not play its home games in New York City. ∎

Yogi sports his familiar batting stroke during a workout as the Astros' new coach. (News photo by Vincent Riehl.)

Astros After Yogi as a Lanier Coach

by Bill Madden

It isn't often a club calls a news conference to announce its manager one week and follows up with an even bigger news conference to announce a coach a week later. But this scenario appears to be unfolding in Houston, with Yogi Berra expected to soon join the Astros as the top lieutenant for Hal Lanier, who was named Astros manager yesterday.

Berra has departed on a week-long cruise. He has informed Yankee officials he is not interested in returning to the Bronx as Lou Piniella's bench coach and let it be known that he would probably accept a similar position in Houston. Berra's Houston connection is Astros owner John McMullen, who was unsuccessful in talking Yogi into managing the Astros.

"John's too good a friend and I want it to remain that way," Yogi explained.

So, in all likelihood, it will be Yogi in those garish rainbow Astro doubleknits as a coach next year. It may not look right to anyone except maybe the fans in Houston. But that's McMullen's prime objective in luring Yogi to Texas. Until now, the Astros have been a colorless (except for their uniforms), faceless team. Next year, their most recognizable face will, in all probability, be the guy sitting next to Lanier.

"I'm really hopeful this thing can happen," McMullen said yesterday. "One reason it's taking so long is we wanted to get permission from the Yankees and make certain Yogi was completely free and clear of any ties there. I can't think of a classier addition to our ball club than Yogi Berra will be." ■

Yogi Legend

During one of his many trips to St. Louis, Yogi was interviewed on a radio show by fellow Hall of Famer Cardinal broadcaster Jack Buck. All guests on Buck's show were given a small check as a token of appreciation for being on the show. So that Buck wouldn't need a special check for every guest, he carried a number of checks made out simply to "bearer." Legend has it that when Yogi received his check from Buck, he turned to Jack and said, "You've known me all this time and you still don't know how to spell my name right!"

November 19, 1985

Yogi Gets a Big Welcome From Astros Pilot Lanier

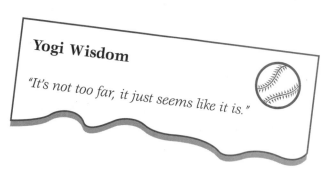

Yogi Wisdom

"It's not too far, it just seems like it is."

Yogi Berra joined the Houston Astros yesterday as a coach, completing manager Hal Lanier's staff.

"He'll be a big asset to our club," said Lanier, named Astros manager Nov. 5. "Yogi has been exposed to every aspect of the game. He has coached first and third base as well as managed."

Berra, 60, skippered the 1964 Yankees and the 1973 Mets to the World Series, making him one of only five managers to represent both leagues in a World Series.

Berra started last season as manager of the Yankees but was relieved with a 6-10 record and replaced by Billy Martin.

The 1986 season will mark his 16th year as a big league coach, having served the Mets from 1965 through 1971 and the Yankees from 1976 to 1983.

"Yogi is a proven winner and an outstanding baseball person," Astros GM Dick Wagner said. "His addition gives the Astros one of the best coaching staffs in all of baseball." ■

Yogi looks right at home in his new uniform. (News photo by Keith Torrie.)

Astro Phenomena

Seeing & speaking to Houston's Yogi

by Phil Pepe

The face is familiar. There is, for sure, only one like it in the world. The No. 8 on the back is also familiar. But the uniform . . . the uniform looks like somebody left a box of crayons in the pockets when it was put in the washer and the colors splattered all over.

Yogi Berra smiles that familiar, toothy, Ernest Borgnine smile when you mention it to him. It is the first time in four decades the name on the uniform does not say "New York," but if you are looking for complaints, if you think you will get grumbling and finger-pointing, then you have come to the wrong place . . . and to the wrong man.

Yogi Berra, now coaching with the Houston Astros, is a happy man, a contented man. It is his rare gift that he can be at home in any place, in any situation; that he holds no grudges.

The sudden, unwarranted firing 16 games into last season by George Steinbrenner stung him deeply. So did some remarks attributed to Billy Martin that seemed to impugn his managerial ability and his preparedness. But Yogi Berra will not retaliate. That is not his way. Yogi Berra's way is to see the good in people or see nothing at all.

The Positive Approach

"We're gonna score some runs," he says. The positive approach. Always the positive approach.

He might have talked about the defensive deficiencies of the Astros or the thin pitching staff. Not Yogi.

"We're gonna score some runs," he says again. "Wait 'til you see this kid at first base [Glenn Davis]. Big. Strong. He can hit. Had three homers the other day."

To Yogi Berra, loyalty never has been a one-way street, and so when Astros owner John McMullen, his good friend, asked him to come aboard as a coach, Berra agreed. But he would not manage.

"Never again," Berra says. "I told John McMullen that."

Perhaps McMullen thought he was doing Berra a favor, giving him a job, keeping him in uniform. Perhaps Berra thought he was doing McMullen a favor, bringing his famous face and name to Houston to help sell some tickets and bringing his years of experience to help get rookie manager Hal Lanier over the hump. It doesn't matter who was doing whom a favor. With friends, it never does. And Yogi is happy to be back in the game.

Back to His Roots

"I'll get to go to St. Louis again," he says. "I haven't been there in years."

St. Louis, of course, is where Berra was born, where he grew up. He has relatives there. And friends.

"I'll get home [Upper Montclair] when we play in New York and Philadelphia," he adds. "One good thing about playing in the Dome, you can make plans. You know you're not going to get rained out. And when there's a day off, you know you're gonna be off."

The last was a veiled reference to Steinbrenner's penchant for turning days off into mandatory workouts. It was the closest Berra would come to putting the knock on the man who fired him in May.

'How's Lou Doing?'

He will continue to follow the Yankees, partly because No. 3 son Dale is still held hostage there, largely because he always will be a Yankee. It is not surprising that upon seeing a visitor from New York, the first thing he asks is, "How are things over there? How's Lou doing?"

If he could give Piniella any advice, it would be to "let it go in here [he pointed to his left ear] and out here [pointing to his right ear]. And one other thing. Win. Don't lose two games in a row."

But he is an Astro now. He has made the transition comfortably.

"We play the Mets in May," Yogi said, "and Carm [wife Carmen] is going to stay home and then come down when we go back to Houston. We got a nice place, right near the Galleria shopping center, but I hope she doesn't spend all her time shopping."

He is 60 now and he does not have to work another day if he doesn't want to, but he cannot stay away from the game. It has been his life for almost 50 years.

'I Love It'

"I love it," he says. "Maybe it's because I always did it, all the way back to American Legion ball. And in the Navy I traveled a lot."

He is a person of such simple tastes. It does not take much to make Yogi Berra happy. ∎

"Wait a minute, these people came all the way from Texas," Yogi reportedly said during a banquet in Houston as he paused to give an autograph to a Dallas couple.

THE YOGI FACTOR

October 1, 1986—As if dealing with the Astros' starting pitching isn't task enough, the Mets will be going up against the "Yogi Berra Factor" in this year's NLCS. The former Yankee legend and current Astro coach has been involved in 21 World Series—14 as a player, five as a coach, and two as a manager. Yog's knack for being in uniform for the Fall Classic is just one of the reasons folks like Met broadcaster Bob Murphy say Berra is one strange-shaped four-leaf clover.

"I remember the late (former Met GM) Bob Scheffing used to say that if he was on a plane that was having trouble, he'd want to be seated with Willie Mays on one side and Yogi Berra on the other. He said that would ensure that he'd walk off the plane without a scratch."

Hey, Hey Yogi!

Astros' Rise Began With Berra

by Phil Pepe

Several reasons have been advanced for the Astros' surprising success: the contribution of rookie manager Hal Lanier; the dramatic improvement of Mike Scott, who clinched the National League West title yesterday with a no-hitter against the Giants; the arrival of Glenn Davis as Houston's first bona fide power hitter since Jimmy Wynn.

But we know the real reason for the Astros' success, those of us who have tracked the career of Lawrence Peter Berra. When the Astros hired Yogi Berra as a coach during the off season, they became favorites to win the National League pennant.

It's called Yogi Luck and it beats four-leaf clovers and horseshoes.

In a career that has spanned four decades, Yogi Berra has cashed 21 World Series checks—14 as a player (a record), four as a Yankees coach, one as a Mets coach, one each as a manager of the Yankees and Mets.

Would anyone bet against him making it 22 this year?

The man has the Midas touch. He got into the bowling business before the boom and sold before the crash. He lent his name to the Yoo-Hoo chocolate drink company and wound up with a vice presidency. Whatever he touches becomes gold.

This happened when Berra was a Mets coach. A laundry in St. Petersburg offered one-day service. One day, manager Gil Hodges, coaches Berra, Joe Pignatano, and Rube Walker left their laundry on the way to the ball park and picked it up on the way home.

"We go in to pick up our laundry," recalled Pignatano. "Gil gives the girl his ticket, gets his laundry, and pays his bill. Rube and I do the same. Now Yogi gives the girl his ticket, gets his laundry, and hands her some money. She rings up the cash register and a star comes up.

"'No charge for you, sir,' she says. 'Every thousandth customer gets his laundry free. That's what the star means.'" ∎

Yogi Berra and Astros slugger Glenn Davis study the Mets' pitching staff for the National League Championship Series. (News photo by Keith Torrie.)

Comeback Mets Capture Flag in 16th

by Phil Pepe

Houston, October 16, 1986—The clock says 6:48 p.m. Central Daylight Time and the Mets and Astros are still playing baseball. They have been playing for four hours and 42 minutes, for 16 innings, making it the longest postseason game in baseball history, and there still is no decision.

The Mets have stomped on the Astros. They have choked them, stepped on them, driven stakes through their heart, held their heads under water, and the Astros are still alive.

The score is 7-6 and the Astros have the tying run on second and the winning run on first and Kevin Bass, their best hitter, is at the plate. There are two out and the count is 3-2 and the prevailing thought is that this game is never going to end. It will go on indefinitely and finally it will have to be ruled a no-decision.

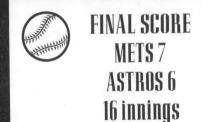

**FINAL SCORE
METS 7
ASTROS 6
16 innings**

But wait. NBC is projecting the Mets the winner. And now the results are official. Jesse Orosco throws another slider. Kevin Bass swings and misses. Orosco claims victory. Bass concedes.

The Mets have finally put down the stubborn Astros in six games.

The Mets are champions of the National League for the first time in 13 years.

In the press box, they are calling it the greatest game ever played. Who's to say? But 45,718 fans in the Astrodome and all the players and coaches and both managers will not dispute the claim.

How many highs and lows can there be in one baseball game? How many times can a team win a game, then lose it, then win it again? How many rides on the emotional roller coaster can one baseball game provide?

How do you measure the unbridled exhilaration of the Mets or the abject disappointment of the Astros? And why does there have to be a loser in a game like this?

You measure this game in heartbeats and comebacks and heroism.

It's Over! Yogi's Hanging 'Em Up

Yogi Berra announced yesterday that he is taking off his uniform at the end of this season . . . It's over.

"I felt in spring training that this might be it," said Berra, a Houston Astros coach the past four years. "I figured after 42 years it was time to try something else."

He will become the Astros' senior baseball adviser. "I've got seven grandkids and I want to see more of them," Berra said. "I want a chance to travel a bit more before I die. If we want to take a trip to Europe, we might just do it."

He put on his first pro baseball uniform in 1943, Norfolk, the Piedmont League, a $500 bonus from the Yankees (but only if he lasted the full season) and $90 a month. The uniform he wore for the next two years belonged to the Navy.

Graduated to the Yankees in 1946, he played 2,116 games in pinstripes. Hall of Fame in 1972. Three-time American League MVP, 14 World Series, 18 All-Star games, 358 homers. Yogi managed the Yankees in 1964, lost the World Series in seven games, and was fired. He joined the Mets for a few at-bats in 1965, coached, became the manager in 1972, won a pennant the next year, and lost another World Series in seven games.

Returning to coach the Yanks in 1976, he managed them to third place in 1984 and was canned 16 games into the following year. When he took off a New York uniform for the first time in 40 seasons, he joined the Astros as a coach.

"I couldn't ask for anything else from my career," Berra said. "This had nothing to do with anything that happened during the season. I had said I'd take it one year at a time."

Yesterday, after four years with Houston, and four months past his 64th birthday, Yogi said he was done. Lawrence Peter (Yogi) Berra will be out of uniform. ■

One of Yogi's "retirement" activities will be to work on his golf game. Here, he is shown teeing off at his own charity event in Montclair, N.J. to benefit handicapped Boy Scouts. (News photo by Joe DeMaria.)

"Why buy good luggage? You only use it when you travel"
—Since Yogi and Carmen plan to do some traveling now that Yogi has
hung up his gloves, it might be a good time for some new luggage.

"The future ain't what it used to be."

News photo by Walter Kelleher

1990 to the Present

Yogi's retirement at the end of the 1989 season lowered the curtain on a professional baseball career that spanned 47 years.

Although Yogi left baseball, he did not leave the spotlight. He remains one of the best-known and most beloved figures in sports, in New York and in the United States. He is far from reclusive and continues to attend Hall of Fame ceremonies and many other events. In May 1996, his hometown university, Montclair State, awarded Yogi and Bruce Willis honorary degrees, and Yogi took advantage of the opportunity to impart his unique wisdom to the graduates. The university is the site of the new Yogi Berra Stadium, home of the university's baseball team as well as a minor league team. The school also houses the Yogi Berra Museum, a 4,000-square-foot facility chronicling Yogi's rise to national fame.

Yogi's baseball career does not define his personality; it is merely a facet. And while his life in baseball may be over, the rest of his life has barely begun. ■

Yogi Berra, Mrs. Mantle, and Earl Monroe attend a kickoff event to assist Mickey's Team in support of organ donation programs across the country. (News photo by Dan Farrell.)

May 17, 1996

Call Him Dr. Yogi

He Grins & Berras Ceremony

by Filip Bondy

Yogi Berra looked good yesterday in the black cap and gown, better than you would expect. He didn't trip on the robe, or any words. The malapropisms in his speech, the Yogiisms, were deliberate.

The notion of Yogi getting an honorary doctorate from Montclair State sounded funnier than the reality, because there was enough dignity in the man to carry off the garb, and the title.

"I don't know yet whether people should call me 'Dr. Yogi' or 'Dr. Lawrence,'" Berra said after graduation ceremonies at Meadowlands Arena. "I'm going to phone Bobby Brown and tell him I'm a doctor, too."

Dr. Yogi.

Let George Steinbrenner chew on that for a while.

"All the money Steinbrenner's donated, he's probably a doctor, too," Berra moaned.

Berra, 71, never came closer than about 11 years of homework and final exams to this sort of scholastic honor in his former life. He is an unschooled, decent man defined by the toughest of beginnings.

He grew up on Elizabeth St. in St. Louis, in the neighborhood known as The Hill. He made it through grade school, and no more. There wasn't time.

"My parents were from the old country," Berra said. "They didn't know about baseball or college. I

Former Montclair neighbors Bruce Willis and Yogi Berra were honorary-degree recipients at the Montclair State University commencement exercises held at the Continental Arena in the Meadowlands. (News photo by Keith Torrie.)

had to go to work. I got a permit when I was 15 to work in a shoe factory."

He fought in World War II. Then came baseball, the Yankees, for 19 years, 14 World Series, 10 titles, and three MVP seasons. Berra never went back to classes. He didn't need a high school degree to play catcher.

"I liked arithmetic best," he said. "Figuring things out. I tried to use it managing."

Yesterday, Berra was on the lectern, reading homemade text to the graduating class from his adopted hometown in North Jersey. He was a big hit, along with another honorary doctoral candidate, Bruce Willis, a Montclair State dropout.

The MSU president, Irvin Reid, gave him the degree of doctor of humane letters, commending Berra for his "ability to combine words with a common-sense philosophy that is easily understood despite its creative expressions."

Berra insisted again he never knew he was being funny when he was being funny. "I really didn't say everything I said," he said.

During his speech, he offered five tips to graduating seniors:

"First, never give up, 'cause it ain't over till it's over.

"Second, when you come to that fork in the road, take it.

"Third, don't always follow the crowd. Nobody goes there because it's too crowded.

"Fourth, stay alert. You observe a lot just by watching.

"Fifth, remember that whatever you do in life, 90% of it is half mental."

The words were culled from a lifetime of unintentional and sometimes painful language dismemberment. Berra has learned to allow outsiders to take their liberties with him. It is harmless fun if he can join in. He has a face that makes people smile, and an image that makes them laugh.

After years of self-doubt, he has become a tremendous sport about all of it.

Berra was never the natural cutup that some people seemed to expect when they met him, pestering him for a one-liner. He is always polite and obliging. But Berra doesn't enjoy speaking to strangers, and he was actually one of the tougher quotes as a manager.

Many of the quips attributed to him weren't really his. But there were genuine, inspirational moments, if you happened to be there.

There was the time he greeted the holiest of holy men with a simple "Hello, Pope."

There was the time Mary Lindsay, wife of the former New York mayor, wondered aloud at Berra's ability to stay cool and crisp on a steaming city day.

"You don't look so hot yourself," Berra told her.

Back in spring training in Fort Lauderdale, 1983, I was lucky enough to hear a Yogiism firsthand. Billy Martin was the manager. Berra was a coach, Mickey Mantle an instructor.

After practice one day, the three were talking about what they were going to do that night. They didn't have many ideas, so Mantle finally said, "There's a good Steve McQueen movie on television tonight—*Bullitt*."

Berra looked a bit confused at this. "I never heard of it," he said. "McQueen must have made that one before he died."

Like the best Berraisms, this one made sense and nonsense at the same time.

He was at it again yesterday, when he and Willis reminisced about how they once lived next to each other on Highland Ave. in Montclair.

"He was the perfect neighbor," Berra said. "Never said a word."

Good line, but not quite a Yogiism. Too practiced.

"I wish I could say them when I wanted to, because I'd have made a fortune by now," he said.

Berra is a mainstay in Montclair, where he reads stories to children at library functions and helps at fund-raisers.

His wife, Carmen, was there yesterday at the arena. So were Berra's three sons and several of his seven grandchildren, all of whom will receive better educations than the family patriarch. Lawrence (Larry) Berra Jr. graduated from Montclair State in 1974.

His father, the doctor, is no dummy, either. ■

May 2, 1997

On This Field, Yogi's Boss

by Filip Bondy

Yogi Berra leaned over the site yesterday of a proposed $10 million stadium that will bear his name and nurture his favorite sport. He threw a ceremonial pitch onto the ground already torn open by bulldozers, at the north end of the Montclair State University campus in New Jersey.

Sweet irony wasn't foremost in his mind on this spring day. But Yogi was sharp enough to understand the implications.

Berra was going to get his stadium in New Jersey. George Steinbrenner was not.

"I don't know about that," Berra mused, when he was asked whether Steinbrenner would be welcome at Yogi Berra Stadium when it opens next spring. "I guess it's up to him if he wants to come."

Yogi will not go to Yankee Stadium for Old-Timers' Day games, or for any other function, as long as Steinbrenner is the club owner. He has kept his word on that, all these years. But he is willing to play host to The Boss on his very own turf.

Berra has always been a gracious winner since he was collecting pennants playing and managing in New York. Now he's won a different competition

against the man who fired him for Billy Martin ridiculously early in the 1985 season. Berra has won the stadium race.

His new place will be home to Montclair State's baseball team in the spring, and to a Class A independent minor league team in the summer. It will seat 3,500 fans, among whom Berra, a Montclair resident, promised to be counted from time to time. The stadium will have natural grass, which is the only specification requested by Berra.

He also hoped this new stadium, 310 feet down the line, would be a good hitter's field.

"I always liked Detroit," he said. "A great park to hit in. You could see the ball great, into the background."

The project, which eventually will include a new ice rink and softball fields, was funded with money from Floyd Hall Enterprises, of Kmart fame,

Yogi Berra Stadium at Montclair State University was officially opened on June 5, 1998. (News photo by Robert Rosamilio.)

Montclair State, and the New Jersey Educational Facilities Authority.

Originally, when the project was at its earliest stages, there was some discussion in planning groups about seeking a donation from Steinbrenner.

"Then we figured, 'No way, if it's Yogi,'" one organizer said yesterday.

The building is a relatively modest construction by today's megastandards. User-friendly and affordable, an investment like this makes so much more sense than anything the state of New Jersey ever thought of doing for Steinbrenner. This field will be enjoyed by players and spectators on the local level. It will not be used as blackmail or leverage.

Left to right at the Stadium dedication ceremonies are Kmart CEO Floyd Hall, Dr. Irvin Reid, president of Montclair State University, Yogi Berra, and Murry Cole. (News photo by Robert Rosamilio.)

"It'll be fun to see some young kids playing out here," Berra said. "If I'm still alive, I'll come."

The New Jersey flirtation with Steinbrenner, meanwhile, appears at death's door. Alan Steinberg, assistant commissioner of the state's Department of Commerce and Economic Development, declined yesterday to comment on the matter.

But the rumors have ended. Where there is no smoke, there is generally no stadium. Where there is no viable alternative, there is no reason for Mayor Giuliani to spend $1 billion to clog the West Side of Manhattan.

"I'd like to see them fix up Yankee Stadium in the Bronx, the same way they built that stadium in Baltimore," Berra said, getting in his nudge. "That would be great. That stadium's got such tradition."

This was a new experience for Berra, a building in his honor. When he was a kid in St. Louis, he played his baseball in Berra Park and his family lived on Berra St. But those were named after a different Berra, a politician.

"No relation," Yogi said. "Didn't even know him."

When he got older, he opened the Berra bowling alley on Route 3 in nearby Clifton. Fun for a while,

but Berra sold the place.

The college came to him about a year ago with this project idea. Hall's money made it all work.

"It will be a place for youngsters who dream of becoming the next Yogi Berra," said university president Irvin Reid at the ground-breaking ceremony. "It represents the best of public and private partnerships."

Berra was honored by the honor.

"During my career, I played in many stadiums with famous names," Berra said. "I played at Fenway Park, at Ebbets Field, and at Comiskey Park. I managed at Shea and at the Astrodome. I also played in a stadium they called 'The House That Ruth Built.'

"Now I have my name on a stadium, too," Berra said. "It makes me very proud."

Berra's speech did not contain a single malapropism, a vaunted Yogiism. It fell upon the stadium architect, Terry Parker, to put that final touch on the day, when asked about the construction timetable.

"It ain't built 'til it's built," Parker said.

Yogi at Yogi Berra Stadium, in New Jersey. The Yankees at Yankee Stadium, in the Bronx.

On a perfect baseball day in Montclair, that arrangement sounded about right. ■

Yogi's From Era of Fan-tastic Baseball

by Mike Lupica

At a time in sports when the owners and athletes seem to want it all and get it all, there is this baseball weekend at Shea Stadium between the Mets and Yankees, and it is all for the fans.

It is all from another time and a better time, when baseball was everything here and people rooted for their team and their players and somehow felt as if they were all in it together. When the best baseball you could ever see really did seem to be available for the price of a subway token, to Yankee Stadium or the Polo Grounds or Ebbets Field.

"I took the subway to the World Series, sure," Yogi Berra was saying in the Mets dugout Friday night, less than five minutes before he would throw out the first pitch of this summer Subway Series at Shea. "I was like everybody else."

The Mets were all in the dugout now, in uniform, ready to go. They kept coming over to where Yogi sat near the bat rack, carrying pens and new baseballs, politely asking him to sign. Todd Pratt, a backup catcher, came over, introduced himself, shyly handed Yogi a ball. So did Alberto Castillo, another Mets catcher. Like kids. Like kids in Mets caps from high up in the bleachers. Everybody is a fan this weekend. Everybody is a kid.

Baseball still matters here this weekend. It is still the best memories, especially here. Yogi is a bridge to more memories than anyone. It was all there for you to see Friday night. The game is ready to start, and he has turned the Mets dugout into a signing at a card show.

"After I was married," he was saying, "we used to drive in to the Stadium, and the players and wives would take a couple of special buses when we'd go over and play the Dodgers a Series game at Ebbets Field. But in October of '47, some of us stayed at the Edison Hotel. Me and Frank Shea and Don Johnson took the subway over to Brooklyn."

The old man shook his head at a memory of his own. His head is full of them. Castillo came over with another baseball for him to sign.

"Man," Yogi Berra said. "All them stops along the way."

He was asked if he knew how to get to Brooklyn on the subway himself in those days. Shook his head.

"Shea did," he said.

He has made all the stops now. From his old battery mate, Spec Shea, who won two games for the Yankees in that '47 Subway Series, to this Mets-Yankees series at Shea Stadium more than a half-century later.

Mike Piazza, who is supposed to get $100 million to stay with the Mets after this season, came over in full catcher's equipment to shake Yogi Berra's hand. He seemed to be twice Berra's size. Somehow, though, maybe because of the magic of the night, some trick of the ballpark light in the early evening, Piazza seemed to be the one looking up, at a ballplayer out of New York's baseball past, one of those giants of the past, before the million-dollar contracts, who rode the subway with the fans and somehow tricked them into believing they would have played these games for free.

These three games between the Mets and Yankees are about that connection. We do not have to talk about new billion-dollar stadiums in New York this weekend. The people lucky enough to have tickets sit in old Shea Stadium and imagine even older ballparks two of them long gone.

"It was like this," Yogi said. "Something would happen in the game, and you wondered who the home team was."

It was like that at Shea in Game One. If you were getting something to eat or drink, and a cheer would explode from inside, you couldn't read whether a Met had done something, or a Yankee. Yesterday was different, all Yankees from the start. This time it was Tino Martinez hitting a three-run homer to turn things around for the Yankees, who seem more interested at this point in world domination than a mere city championship. The night before it was Paul O'Neill hitting the big three-run homer for the Yankees and making Shea in June sound more like Yankee Stadium in October.

"I'm glad we're at Shea," O'Neill said after Friday's game, talking about his shot over the wall in left-center. "That ball wouldn't have made it out at the Stadium."

Everybody at Shea seemed glad to be there, even after a couple of Yankee blowout victories. But those who aren't there, who are watching or listening on the radio the way people once listened to Red Barber and Mel Allen, still feel as if they are going to these games.

This is the weekend when New York feels as if it has gone to a baseball game.

At 7:35 Friday night, to start it off, was Yogi. Who else? He is the Yankees vs. the Dodgers in '47, Jackie Robinson driving him nuts on the bases.

"I was young," he said Friday. "Jackie was real good." He is five straight World Series between '49 and '53. He is a Yankee from DiMaggio to Mantle. He is Larsen's perfect game, and the Yankee manager in the '64 Series and the Mets manager in the '73 Series, that summer at Shea, somehow 25 years ago now, when it wasn't over till it was over. He had a Mets cap, black with a blue bill, in his left hand, saying it would make a real nice golf cap.

A brand-new white baseball in that old catcher's right hand.

Somebody told him it was time to throw out the first pitch to Piazza, like some throw from all the way back with him, even past the '50s, out of that World Series in 1947, to which he traveled by subway with Spec Shea.

"I'm gonna have to cheat like hell to get this ball to home plate," he said, and then walked up out of the dugout at Shea Stadium and into the big New York baseball night, almost as big as he remembered. ■

Mel Allen and Yogi Berra bat the pregame breeze during an era when baseball was king. Thanks, in part, to the record-setting performance of the 1998 Yankees, baseball has once again taken its place as America's favorite pastime.

"I really didn't say everything I said."
— Maybe not, but America sure has observed a lot just by listening.